HERE COMES ANOTHER EXCITING BASKETBALL SEASON!

And this is the perfect book to help you follow all the action. It includes, for each NBA team, expert prediction, statistics, roster, our own Performance Quotient rating system—and such special features as:

- Action profiles of NBA stars
- Exclusive feature stories
- Highlights of the '77 playoffs
- Official records section
- Action photos of stars of every team

All of this in
PRO BASKETBALL '77-'78
A Ballantine Original

Don't miss the other exciting books in this series
published by Ballantine Books:

MAJOR LEAGUE BASEBALL 1977
PRO FOOTBALL 1977
HOCKEY '77-'78

available at your local bookstore

PRO BASKETBALL '77-'78

in association with

Talisman Books, Inc.

illustrated

BALLANTINE BOOKS • NEW YORK

Copyright © 1977 by Talisman Books, Inc.

All rights reserved under International and
Pan-American Copyright Conventions.

Published in the United States by Ballantine Books,
a division of Random House, Inc., New York,
and simultaneously in Canada by
Ballantine Books of Canada, Ltd., Toronto, Canada.

ISBN 0-345-25823-1

Manufactured in the United States of America

First Edition: October 1977

CREDITS:

Writing by Martin Lader and Chris Scherf.

Cover photograph of Julius Erving of the Philadelphia 76ers by Carl Skalak, Jr./Opticom Photographic Services.

Inside photos by Steve Snodgrass, Nancy Hogue, Malcolm W. Emmons, George Gojkovich, Sue Cassidy Clark, Jim Anderson, Eileen Miller, Ronald C. Modra and Wide World Photos.

Contents

ACTION PHOTO GALLERIES

The NBA East—MVPs and All-Stars............56
The NBA West—MVPs and All-Stars..........152

THE NATIONAL BASKETBALL ASSOCIATION

Introduction..................................3

EASTERN CONFERENCE

Atlantic Division

Philadelphia 76ers.....5
Boston Celtics........11
New York Knicks....17
Buffalo Braves........23
New Jersey Nets.....29

Central Division

Washington Bullets...35
Houston Rockets.....41
Cleveland Cavaliers...47
New Orleans Jazz.....53
San Antonio Spurs....59
Atlanta Hawks.......65

WESTERN CONFERRENCE

Midwest Division

Denver Nuggets......71
Chicago Bulls........77
Detroit Pistons.......83
Kansas City Kings....89
Milwaukee Bucks.....95
Indiana Pacers......101

Pacific Division

Portland Trail
　Blazers..........107
Los Angeles Lakers..113
Golden State Warriors 119
Seattle SuperSonics..125
Phoenix Suns.......131

SUPER FEATURES

The Free Agent Finds:	If at First...	...139
Walton vs. Jabbar:	Rivalry with Respect	143
Freshmen Pros:	The Cream of the Crop	...153
ABA Survivors:	An Embarrassment of Riches	...163
What's Going on Here?	Unhappiness at the Top	..181
The '77 Playoffs:	Blazer Glory	193

ACTION PROFILES

Julius Erving:	The Doctor Was Out	149
Dave Cowens:	Enthusiasm Regained	159
Moses Malone:	At Home in Houston	172
Bobby Jones:	Computer's Choice	176
Bob McAdoo:	Knicks and Knocks	188

HALL OF RECORDS 211

THE NATIONAL BASKETBALL ASSOCIATION

Complete roster, official statistics, analysis, prediction and Performance Quotient rating system for each NBA team

The NBA in '77-'78

On the pages that follow, this season's 22 NBA entries are evaluated in the most comprehensive and informative format you'll find available.

Each of the teams gets an in-depth analysis; its strengths and weaknesses are examined in relation to the team's performance last season, its potential for the 1977-78 season and the strongpoints and weakpoints of the other teams in its division.

This is followed by the team's personnel depth chart. It includes the names and significant statistics of all of the team's veteran players. You should know the abbreviations used to head each column of statistics: From the left, they are **G** for Games Played; **M** for Minutes Played; **FGM** for Field Goals Made; **FTM** for Free Throws Made; **PTS** for Points Scored; **AVG** for Per Game Scoring Average; **FG%** for Per Cent of Field Goals Made; **REB** for Rebounds; and **ASST** for Assists. The figures shown on the same line as the player's name are his statistics for last year, the 1976-77 season; those shown on the line below—the line that has on it the number of years he has played in the NBA (or ABA) prior to last season—are his career statistics (not including those of the last campaign).

Following this statistical analysis of the players is a listing and appraisal of the most promising rookies who will attempt to help the team in the coming season.

Lastly, each team is assigned a Performance Quotient in each of three important areas—offense, defense and rebounding. The mathematical rating system is based on a top-quality rating of 1, which stands for best or tied for best in that category in the league. A rating of 2 stands for excellent, 3 equals good, 4 is for fair and 5 is poor.

The team with the lowest aggregate Performance Quotient should be the best in its division, but in making our predictions, we have considered a club's intangibles, too. As you will see, the teams appear in the order in which we predict they will finish the season. The Atlantic Division shows the Philadelphia 76ers and the Boston Celtics finishing 1-2. The Washington Bullets and the Houston Rockets should finish first and second, respectively, in the Central Division. Denver's Nuggets and Chicago's Bulls are our choices for first and second finishers in the Midwest Division. And the reigning champion Portland Trail Blazers and the Los Angeles Lakers are our picks to finish first and second in the Pacific Division.

Of the playoff teams, we predict that the 76ers and the Lakers will survive the eliminations and face each other in the final round of the playoffs.

Okay, now it's time to start comparing your selections with ours.

Atlantic Division

Philadelphia 76ers

Prediction: First

The Philadelphia 76ers have been viciously and unjustly maligned. There was a season-long criticism of the team which culminated in one loud harangue when the 76ers lost the National Basketball Association's championship series to the Portland Trail Blazers. Ordinarily, just reaching the NBA finals is regarded as a great achievement, but it wasn't enough for the 76ers' army of critics. No, they were supposed to win the whole thing, just because they had much more talent than anyone else.

Just because 76ers owner John Dixon spent $6.5-million before the season to acquire and pay Julius Erving, maybe the best and certainly the most flamboyant player in basketball, Philadelphia was expected to win the championship. Just because the 76ers already had George McGinnis, who had made the NBA's All-Star team in his first year in the league, at the other forward position and just because they had an outstanding guard in Doug Collins and just because the team had several other extremely talented players: Is that any reason for criticism?

What the critics failed to take into account was the extreme difficulty, even impossibility, of the 76ers' task.

No team ever had every player average 20 points a game, but the 76ers were expected to win the championship as well. Obviously, the 76ers could not do both, so they turned their attention to the more important of the two objectives—everyone averaging 20 points. After all, that's never been done; some team wins the NBA championship every year.

Although only Erving and McGinnis succeeded in averaging more than 20 points a game, it wasn't because of a lack of effort on the part of the other players. The NBA's 24-second clock could have been reduced to 12 seconds and it would not have affected the 76ers' style of play. While the critics unmercifully attack the 76ers' no-pass offense, they overlook the tremendous success Woody Hayes and Bo Schembechler have had with it. The 76ers simply were using the offense best suited to their personnel and in Lloyd Free they had the perfect man to run it. All season long, Free brilliantly used Erving and McGinnis as decoys, but all he got for his efforts was unending criticism.

Although the 76ers might have been humbled by losing the championship series to Portland in six games, many Philadelphia players proved they didn't know the meaning of the word humble.

"Just because we lost doesn't mean we're dead," said 20-year-old center Darryl Dawkins, who remained unfazed by the fact the Trail Blazers had swept the 76ers in the final four games of the series.

Coach Gene Shue may have been one of the 76ers' problems. "I have a group of very strong-willed individual players," he said after the season ended. "This has not been the easiest team to coach."

However, it should have been the easiest team in basketball history to coach. All he had to do was sit back and shut up. And his players kept telling him that.

But he persisted in trying to get the 76ers to function as a unit rather than five individuals.

Is it any wonder Erving had to give this assessment after the title series: "We were consistent all year— consistently unpredictable."

Erving, who averaged 21.6 points a game during the regular season, was forced to demonstrate why so many consider him the best player in basketball when his great teammates suddenly became not-so-great in the final series against Portland. An extremely considerate group, the 76ers had not called upon Erving to expend his remarkable talents during the regular season. But when an emergency arose and the 76ers began to look like a terminal case, they suddenly started to call on Dr. J.

Erving, whose wife Turquoise had joined the 76ers' critics during the season, refused to join the chorus after the loss to Portland.

"If we start off next year as a blackboard team, who's to say we'll be better," Erving said. "We might be worse. We aren't a blackboard team. We don't play by the book. Who's to say the book is better for us?"

But McGinnis, for one, would like to change the script. "One thing we definitely learned, we definitely have to stick together," said McGinnis, who averaged 21.4 points and 11.5 rebounds a game during the regular season before going into a horrible slump in the playoffs. "We fought each other all year. There were a lot of things said. It just caused us a lot of problems that could have been avoided. I think we all grew up.

"I think we had a tendency to cut corners because of our talent. We were so talented, we didn't feel we had to do a lot of things other teams did."

Collins averaged 18.3 points a game and Free 16.3

to indicate the type of talent the 76ers had at guard. Henry Bibby also averaged 10.2 points from the backcourt.

Steve Mix again proved a valuable reserve forward by averaging 10.5 points despite having his playing time reduced substantially by the addition of Erving.

Caldwell Jones, a 6-11 center from the ABA, was unique among the 76ers for his devotion to defense and rebounding, but his season was a bit of a disappointment. The mammoth Dawkins, though, gave some indication he may soon become as destructive a force on the court as he is in the locker room.

The 76ers' first choice in the college draft was Seton Hall's slender 6-9 Glenn Mosley, the nation's leading rebounder with an average of 16.31 a game.

Mosley "has great quickness, can play inside, or come out and shoot," Shue enthuses. He made more than 50 per cent of his own shots his last two college seasons and blocked a lot of other people's. His college coach, Bill Raftery, feels Mosley, who won't be 22 until midseason, is at least two years away from reaching his full potential and can be an outstanding forward on a running team like the 76ers. Mosley missed the last 14 games of his soph season and first seven as a junior when the NCAA suspended him because of a recruiting technicality. Philadelphia also picked two other big men in the draft, Old Dominion's Wilson Washington and Arizona's Bob Elliott. Then they tried to fill a more pressing need by drafting Oral Roberts' Arnold Dugger, a guard willing to pass the ball.

PREDICTION: FIRST

Statistics for 1976-77 season

Player's name Years in NBA prior to 1976-77	G	M	FGM	FTM	Career statistics, not including those of the 1976-77 season PTS	AVG	FG%	REB	ASST
Bibby, Henry (4 years)	81	2639	302	221	825	10.2	.430	273	356
Bryant, Joe (1 year)	275	4633	824	483	2131	7.7	.431	531	561
Catchings, Harvey (2 years)	61	612	107	53	267	4.4	.446	117	48
Collins, Doug (3 years)	75	1203	552	233	558	7.4	.442	278	61
Dawkins, Darryl (1 year)	53	864	62	33	157	3.0	.504	234	30
Dunleavy, Mike	112	2259	144	74	362	3.2	.456	673	84
	58	2037	426	210	1062	18.3	.518	195	271
	183	6251	1247	758	3252	17.8	.491	668	444
	59	684	135	40	310	5.3	.628	230	24
	37	165	41	8	90	2.4	.500	49	3
	32	359	60	34	154	4.8	.414	34	56
Erving, Julius †(5 years)	82	2940	685	400	1770	21.6	.499	695	306
Free, Lloyd (1 year)	407	16,550	4581	2412	11,662	28.7	.509	4924	1952
Furlow, Terry	78	2253	467	334	1268	16.3	.457	237	266
	71	1121	239	112	590	8.3	.488	125	104
	32	174	34	16	84	2.6	.340	39	19
Jones, Caldwell †(3 years)	82	2023	215	64	494	6.0	.507	666	92
McGinnis, George (1 year)	231	8607	1536	575	3652	15.8	.478	3022	453
	79	2769	659	372	1690	21.4	.458	911	302
	77	2946	647	475	1769	23.0	.417	967	359

PHILADELPHIA 76ERS

	G	M	FGM	FTM	PTS	AVG	FG%	REB	ASST
Mix, Steve	75	1958	288	215	791	10.5	.523	376	152
(6 years)	270	8867	1370	772	3512	13.0	.478	2277	520

†—ABA totals

Most Promising Rookies: Glenn Mosley, Wilson Washington. The 76ers obtained the nation's No. 1 rebounder in Mosley. The 6-foot-8, 196-pounder averaged 16.3 rebounds a game for Seton Hall. The only thing which could stop him from becoming a fine pro player is his slender build. The 6-9 Washington weighs 227 pounds and was Old Dominion's top rebounder as well as its leading scorer. Mosley also is a big offensive threat.

PERFORMANCE QUOTIENTS

Offense: If the 76ers have a problem, it's that they have too much offense. Erving and McGinnis are as great a pair of offensive forwards as any team ever has had. Erving averaged 21.6 points a game and McGinnis 21.4. The guard combination of Collins and Free is an explosive one, too, Collins averaged 18.3 points and Free 16.3. But problems arose as Free never overly concerned himself with working the ball inside to Erving and McGinnis. Ideally, the 76ers should get more scoring from their trio of centers, Jones, Dawkins and Catchings. On the other hand, if they shoot more that means even less shots for Erving and McGinnis. Bibby, Mix and Bryant provide the 76ers with a lot of scoring potential from the bench. Perf. Qt.: 2.

Defense: Overall, the 76ers' defense was embarrassing in the playoffs. Erving and McGinnis do not concentrate solely on offense, although they obviously are being paid for their ability to put points on the scoreboard. Erving's shot-blocking ability can be as awesome as some of his offensive maneuvers. McGinnis likes to gamble on defense and that's why he led the 76ers in steals. But he also gets burned, which is why the addition of a shot-blocker like Jones was so important. Jones' defense would be truly outstanding if he had a bit more bulk. Collins, a fine all-around player, does a good job defensively, but Free has displayed a marked preference for scoring. Perf. Qt.: 3.

Rebounding: The 76ers ranked third in the NBA in rebounding. McGinnis averaged 11.5 rebounds a game. The massively built forward is a terror under the backboards. With Erving's amazing leaping ability, he also ranks as a top rebounder and the 76ers' combination of centers completes an imposing front line. Perf. Qt.: 2.

Atlantic Division

Boston Celtics

Prediction: Second

The Boston Celtics entered the 1976-77 season as the defending National Basketball Association champions and the prospects of successfully defending it appeared bright with the addition of All-Star forwards Sidney Wicks and Curtis Rowe.

The Celtics, consequently, started the season with six All-Star game performers in Wicks, Rowe, Dave Cowens, John Havlicek, Jo Jo White and Charlie Scott.

Despite the addition of Julius Erving to the Philadelphia 76ers' roster, the Celtics still appeared to have an excellent chance of adding to their championship tradition.

However, some very un-Celtic type things began to happen.

John Havlicek, the player who most epitomizes the Celtics' dynasty and the hustling effort which produced it, held out for more money prior to the season and missed training camp.

Then, nine games into the regular season, the fiercely competitive Cowens suddenly decided to leave the team because his intensity already had gone.

Cowens ended up missing more than 30 games and

his return coincided with a broken arm that sidelined Scott for most of the rest of the season.

Under the NBA's new playoff system, the Celtics found the final two months of the regular season nervous ones indeed as Boston was in a bitter struggle with the New York Knicks and the Cleveland Cavaliers for the final two playoff spots. The two division champs and the four teams with the next best records qualified for the playoffs in each conference. The Celtics finished with a 44-38 record to make the playoffs as the Knicks failed to mount a late season rally.

Once they made the playoffs, though, the Celtics were as troublesome as ever, breezing past San Antonio in the preliminary round and extending the 76ers to seven games before finally being eliminated.

The Celtics had more problems than just the injury to Scott and Cowens' early season vacation. They had the second worst shooting percentage in the league, sinking only 44.5 per cent of their field goal attempts; the New York Nets were the only team to do worse.

On the other hand, the Celtics led the league in rebounding with 4207, despite Cowens' lengthy absence.

These statistics indicate Scott's absence might have been more costly than Cowens'. Wicks and Rowe, who combined to lead UCLA to one of its customary national championships, grabbed a total of 1387 rebounds to offset Cowens' absence.

But, when Scott was out, the backcourt burden fell almost solely on the shoulders of White, whose 3333 minutes of playing time were second only to Washington's Elvin Hayes.

White averaged 19.6 points a game to lead the Celtics and had 492 assists, the seventh highest total in the NBA as the outstanding guard was the only Boston player to finish in the top 10 of any individual offensive statistics.

But, while White did his best to compensate for the sidelined Scott, the Celtics' bench failed to come through with much help.

Kevin Stacom connected on only 41 per cent of his field goal attempts for a meager 5.1 scoring average, and when the Celtics added Bobby Wilson to the roster it was only going from bad to worse, as he shot a miserable 32 per cent.

Consequently, the Celtics relied on "Old Reliable" Havlicek to move into the backcourt with White. And, while the 37-year-old star was second in playing time and averaged 17.7 points a game, he had slowed down just enough that White had to do almost all the ball-handling.

Havlicek, who had a shade more speed and quickness than many opponents as a forward, was at a slight disadvantage against the league's fleet backcourt men.

This and Cowens' absence were major factors in the Celtics' disappointing defensive performance. All those championship banners are hanging from the ceiling of the Boston Garden because the Celtics' defensive pressure was relentless. This commando assault unit became a Celtics trademark, but last season's squad had the fewest steals in the league with only 506. The next lowest total was Cleveland's 579.

When Scott was healthy he averaged 18.2 points a game, while Cowens finished with a 16.4 average. Wicks averaged 15.1 points a game and Rowe 10.1.

But, although Boston General Manager Red Auerbach is considered one of basketball's most astute judges of talent, the Celtics have not done well in the draft the past three years and a lack of bench strength has been the result. Forward Norm Cook, Boston's top pick in the 1976 draft, had only 138 minutes of playing time and center Tom Boswell, the previous year's top choice, averaged only 6.4 points a game. The Celtics' two previous No. 1 picks, Glenn McDonald and Steve Downing, no longer are with the club.

But this year's top pick, North Carolina-Charlotte's 6-9 Cedric "Cornbread" Maxwell, should do a much better job of fulfilling the Celtics' expectations. Maxwell averaged 22.3 points a game as a senior by sinking 64 per cent of his field goal attempts and had a rebounding average of 12.1. The No. 2 pick, Wake Forest's Skip Brown, only 5-11, may provide some direly needed ball-handling depth.

"If your dreams are not extravagant, they will be granted," read the message in the fortune cookie Maxwell's agent, Ron Grinkler, got at dinner on July 17. The next day his client signed a multi-year contract with the Celtics. Terms were not disclosed.

Now Coach Tom Heinsohn hopes Cornbread, a smart cookie who led UNCC to the Final Four in the NCAA championships, will improve the Celtics' fortunes.

Earlier, Heinsohn had improved his own bank account by signing a multi-year pact, ending rumors he might not be retained. Heinsohn, noted for his offense as a player, made a bid to restore the team's defensive reputation by hiring former Celtic teammate Satch Sanders, a defensive specialist, as assistant coach.

Barring injury, the Celtics certainly have the personnel to add one more championship banner to the Boston Garden rafters.

PREDICTION: SECOND

Statistics for 1976-77 season

Career statistics, not including those of the 1976-77 season

Player's name (Years in NBA prior to 1976-77)	G	M	FGM	FTM	PTS	AVG	FG%	REB	ASST
Ard, Jim (6 years)	63	969	96	49	241	3.8	.378	296	53
Boswell, Tom (1 year)	140	1572	196	119	511	3.7	.350	488	88
Cook, Norm	70	1083	175	96	446	6.4	.515	306	85
	35	275	41	14	96	2.7	.441	71	16
	25	138	27	9	63	2.5	.375	27	5
Cowens, Dave (6 years)	50	1888	328	162	818	16.4	.434	697	248
Havlicek, John (14 years)	465	18,772	3772	1328	8872	19.1	.456	7209	1781
Kuberski, Steve (7 years)	79	2913	580	235	1395	17.7	.452	382	400
	1109	40,761	9387	4904	23,678	21.4	.438	7293	5386
	76	860	131	63	325	4.3	.420	209	39
Rowe, Curtis (5 years)	489	7023	1122	543	2787	5.7	.417	1931	299
	79	2190	315	170	800	10.1	.498	563	107
	407	13,954	2232	943	5401	13.3	.486	3256	711
Saunders, Fred (2 years)	68	1051	184	35	403	5.9	.466	223	85
Scott, Charlie (5 years)	86	1205	204	72	480	5.6	.434	290	93
	43	1581	326	129	781	18.2	.444	191	196
	290	10,747	2683	1240	6606	22.8	.447	1218	1444
Stacom, Kevin (2 years)	79	1051	179	46	404	5.1	.409	97	117
White, Jo Jo (7 years)	138	1561	242	97	581	4.2	.443	216	177
	82	3333	638	333	1609	19.6	.429	383	492
	542	20,341	4466	1377	10,309	19.0	.446	2380	2771

BOSTON CELTICS

	G	M	FGM	FTM	PTS	AVG	FG%	REB	ASST
Wicks, Sidney (5 years)	82	2642	464	310	1238	15.1	.458	824	169
	398	15,456	3502	1878	8882	22.3	.460	4086	1647

Most Promising Rookies: Cedric Maxwell, Skip Brown. Cornbread Maxwell sank 64 per cent of his shots during his senior year at North Carolina-Charlotte to average 22.3 points a game. The 6-9 Maxwell played center in leading UNCC to the final four of the NCAA tournament. He averaged 12.1 rebounds a game and also displayed outstanding ball-handling ability. He should be the Celtics' best rookie since Paul Westphal. Brown is an excellent all-around guard, but his 5-11 size may prove too much of a handicap to overcome.

PERFORMANCE QUOTIENTS

Offense: The only team with a worse shooting percentage than the Celtics was the New York Nets. Of course, the Celtics' offense was missing two key cogs for much of the season in Cowens and Scott. White led the Celtics in scoring with an average of 19.6. But the fact he had to pick up a lot of the offensive slack was reflected by his shooting percentage of .429. While Scott was healthy he averaged 18.2 points a game, so the pair obviously give the Celtics a potent backcourt. Cowens averaged 16.4 points and Havlicek continued to defy the advancing years by averaging 17.7. The Celtics picked up the former UCLA tandem of Wicks and Rowe to become six deep in All-Stars. Wicks had a 15.1 average and Rowe 10.1. The Boston bench was embarrassingly short on offensive support, but Cedric Maxwell should help the situation. Perf. Qt.: 3.

Defense: The Celtics fell off defensively, but that must be expected when Cowens takes off for 30 games. White led the Celtics in steals with only 118, which was not what would be expected from Boston's famed hustling defense and full-court pressure. Wicks and Rowe do not have reputations as defensive wizards, but they do a good job. Havlicek gets by on hustle, but that wasn't enough when he was forced to turn in long stretches at guard. Scott's return should strengthen the Celtics there, although he's not known as a particularly good defensive player. Perf. Qt.: 3.

Rebounding: Cowens, Wicks and Rowe give the Celtics an extremely strong front line, one able to rebound with anyone, and Maxwell will help. Perf. Qt.: 2.

Atlantic Division

New York Knicks

Prediction: Third

To those who were there, it was the most emotional moment they're ever likely to witness on a basketball court.

It was the night of May 8, 1970, and a sellout crowd of 19,500 was squeezed into Madison Square Garden to witness the seventh game of the championship series between the New York Knicks and Los Angeles Lakers. The Knicks, charter members of the league, still were seeking their first title, but it appeared they'd have to do it without their captain, Willis Reed.

Reed had suffered a painful hip injury early in the fifth game, and even the New York players accepted the fact that he wouldn't be able to play. But Reed, boosted by a 200-milligram shot of carbocaine, ran onto the court just moments before the game began, touching off a tumultuous ovation.

The courageous center then scored his team's first four points and did an effective job of defending Wilt Chamberlain in the 27 minutes he was able to play, and the Knicks had their championship.

"He gave us a tremendous psychological lift," said Walt Frazier, who scored 36 points and added 19 assists in that contest. "When he made that first one, that gave us the momentum we needed."

Recalled Bill Bradley, "He came onto the court at just the right time. It was the perfect psychological move. When I heard the crowd yelling I almost felt like I should do that too. He played on courage, that's all you can say."

Courageous is a perfect adjective to describe Willis Reed. If you're looking for the right cliché, you might say that he always was able to rise to the occasion. It is more than coincidence that Reed captained the Knicks the only two times they won the NBA championship, and that on both occasions he was voted the playoff MVP.

Now Reed returns to the Knicks as coach, and times are almost as bad for them as they were when Reed the player first joined them in 1964. At that time the Knicks had finished in fourth place five consecutive years, and now New York has failed to play .500 ball three years in a row. It isn't mere coincidence that those are the three years since Reed retired as a player.

Reed remembers the way it was, and it isn't at all unusual that he would like to shape the kind of team on which he played. To him, it all comes down to one basic concept.

"Basically, the game is defense," Reed said after accepting a three-year contract for an annual salary reported to be $125,000. "It was the tradition of the New York Knickerbockers and what they became known for. We're going to have to spend a lot of time together, and learn to get it right.

"This team wasn't helping each other out on defense enough. They scored enough points to win, but players have to be willing to attain a common goal. In skills the players today are better than when I was a player, but they are unwilling to sacrifice their individual skills, goals and glory for the good of the team."

New York, which always prided itself on defense under former Coach Red Holzman, allowed 108.6 points per game last season, the fifth poorest figure in the league and the team's highest yield since 1968.

With the retirement of Bradley, the only one left who played on both championship teams is Frazier, and he proved to be a problem last season when he went into a shell. Once the most gregarious of all the Knicks, Frazier took exception to the critical notices he was receiving, stopped talking to the press and relinquished his team captaincy.

The record shows that Frazier, now 32, suffered through his poorest season since his rookie year of 1967-68. He averaged 17.4 points a game with 403 assists, and contributed a career low 293 rebounds.

Still, teamed with Earl Monroe, he provides the Knicks with one of the more explosive backcourt units in the game. Monroe, who took over the team captaincy, averaged 19.9 points last season with 366 assists.

The only Knick to outscore Monroe and Frazier was center Bob McAdoo, who averaged 26.7 points after being acquired from Buffalo and ranked fifth in the league in rebounding with a season total of 926. McAdoo is a pure scorer, as attested to by the fact that only four players in NBA history reached the 10,000 point plateau in less than the 358 games required by McAdoo.

However, this isn't the style of play appreciated by Mac's new boss.

"I personally don't like to have players so far out of line offensively," Reed said without making direct reference to McAdoo. "If you have a guy who averages 30 points and then he scores 10 points, you're killed."

Hurting the Knick cause tremendously last season was the leg injury which limited 6-8 Spencer Haywood to 31 games. New York desperately needs his scoring and rebounding help, but it remains to be seen how effective he can be with a nine-inch diagonal scar in his left knee.

One player Reed may enjoy watching is Lonnie Shelton, who at 6-8 and 250 pounds has been compared favorably to his new coach. Shelton, as a rookie, was the only Knick to play in all 82 games, but he didn't make it to the end that often, fouling out 10 times (the rest of the team was disqualified a total of nine times).

"I think he's being called for a lot of fouls he shouldn't be called for," Holzman said last season. "I think his anticipation is so good that they don't expect it and call him for fouls. They don't think he can be so quick without pushing off."

Shelton averaged 11.6 points last season and was second on the team in rebounding (633), steals (125) and blocked shots (98).

For the Knicks to become a legitimate contender, they'll also have to get more help from Jim McMillian and Tom McMillen, both acquired from Buffalo and both of whom failed to score in double figures.

In the first round of the draft, the Knicks chose 6-2 guard Ray Williams of the University of Minnesota. The brother of Golden State's Gus Williams, Ray used to sneak into Madison Square Garden as a kid to watch Reed and Frazier play. Now he is being touted as the eventual successor to Frazier in the New York backcourt.

Williams figures it will be his responsibility to get the ball to the big guys, and he says, "I figure I can do the job. I enjoy getting the people going and the adrenaline flowing. You can do that with a good pass."

PREDICTION: THIRD

Statistics for 1976-77 season

Player's name Years in NBA prior to 1976-77	G	M	FGM	FTM	PTS	AVG	FG%	REB	ASST
Beard, Butch (6 years)	70	1082	148	75	371	5.3	.505	163	144
Burden, Ticky †(1 year)	449	11,137	1720	1044	4484	10.0	.483	1605	1687
	61	608	148	51	347	5.7	.420	66	62
Frazier, Walt (9 years)	71	2181	561	283	1413	19.9	.457	202	131
	76	2687	532	259	1323	17.4	.489	293	403
Haywood, Spencer (6 years)	683	26,308	5204	2886	13,294	19.5	.492	4305	4388
	31	1021	202	109	513	16.5	.450	280	50
Jackson, Phil (9 years)	404	16,048	3773	2134	9680	24.0	.460	4832	861
	76	1033	102	51	255	3.4	.440	229	85
Layton, Mo (3 years)	593	11,250	1746	1089	4581	7.7	.449	2913	670
	56	765	134	58	326	5.8	.484	47	154
*McAdoo, Bob (4 years)	167	3166	546	226	1318	7.9	.432	274	437
	72	2798	740	381	1861	25.8	.512	926	205
*McMillen, Tom (1 year)	314	12,614	3515	1930	8960	28.5	.502	3965	803
	76	1492	274	96	644	8.5	.487	389	67
McMillian, Jim (6 years)	50	708	96	41	233	4.7	.432	186	69
	67	2158	298	67	663	9.9	.464	307	139
Meminger, Dean (5 years)	460	15,814	3025	1249	7299	15.9	.486	2684	1180
	32	254	15	13	43	1.3	.417	26	29
Monroe, Earl (9 years)	384	8300	989	531	2509	6.5	.476	1060	1017
	77	2656	613	307	1533	19.9	.517	223	366
	658	22,585	5247	2908	13,402	20.4	.455	2281	2611

NEW YORK KNICKS

	G	M	FGM	FTM	PTS	AVG	FG%	REB	ASST
Shelton, Lonnie	82	2104	398	159	955	11.6	.476	633	149

- —Combined Buffalo-Knicks totals
- †—ABA totals

Most Promising Rookies: Ray Williams, Glen Gondrezick, Toby Knight. Williams, long a Knick fan, is being looked upon as a playmaker even though the 6-2 guard took down 7.5 rebounds and averaged 18 points last season at the University of Minnesota. He also led the Big 10 in assists and he says, "If the big men are open, I think they deserve to get the ball as long as they are scoring. I think I can call myself an unselfish player." Gondrezick, a 6-6 forward from Nevada-Las Vegas, is not a big scorer but he averaged 10 rebounds a game and is effective on the offensive boards while Knight, a 6-8 forward from Notre Dame, also is a strong rebounder.

PERFORMANCE QUOTIENTS

Offense: Here's a surprise for you: the Knicks were the most accurate shooting team in the NBA last season, hitting on almost 49 per cent of their floor shots, and their average of 108.6 points a game represented an improvement of six points over the previous year. The big change in the New York attack was provided, of course, by the acquisition of McAdoo, the fifth leading scorer in the league with a 25.8 average and a .512 accuracy mark. It will be interesting to see what happens in the new campaign since Coach Willis Reed says it isn't his style to depend on one big scorer. Monroe and Frazier both fell below their career scoring marks, but still provide New York with one of the more dynamic backcourt duos in the game. Haywood managed to score at a 16.5 clip in the 31 games his injured knee allowed him to play, and New York desperately needs a comeback from this big man. **Perf. Qt.: 2.**

Defense: It is more than coincidence that when Reed accepted the coaching position, he stressed the word "defense." That was the byword of the championship teams he played on in New York, and a phase of the game that now seems forgotten. The Knicks yielded 108.6 points last season, a figure that only four other clubs topped. He doesn't like to hear this, but Frazier, once a perennial choice to the All-Defensive team, isn't quite as effective as he was in his younger days. **Perf. Qt.: 4.**

Rebounding: Again, a lot will depend on the availability of Haywood, who would provide the Knicks a strong combination with McAdoo. Only one team had fewer than the 3654 rebounds New York managed and there's no telling how embarrassing the situation would have been were it not for McAdoo's total of 926. Shelton added 633. **Perf. Qt.: 5.**

Atlantic Division

Buffalo Braves

Prediction: Fourth

In considering the plight of the Buffalo Braves, it is far more gratifying to think in terms of what might have been than what is going to be.

What could have been is a front line consisting of such players as Bob McAdoo, Moses Malone, Gar Heard, Elmore Smith, Jim McMillian, Tom McMillen, Steve Kuberski and Kevin Kunnert, not to mention guards such as Herm Gilliam and Ken Charles. All wore Buffalo uniforms at one time, and all were dealt away.

Leading this group of talent might have been Jack Ramsay, who coached the Braves from 1972-76, and last season guided Portland to the NBA championship.

What was left was a disorganized, unhappy group of players, who weren't even sure if the franchise would remain in Buffalo, and a resulting 30-52 record, the second poorest in the league. Not surprisingly, the club failed to qualify for the playoffs for the first time since 1972-73.

Such was the upheaval that 19 players were listed on Buffalo's roster during last season, there were three coaches and a new ownership structure.

"There's been a lot of changes in this franchise," said

Ernie DiGregorio, himself a pawn in the intraclub friction. "There's been different players, there's been different systems, there's been different coaches and there's been different philosophies.

"That's almost impossible to go through a situation like that and continue to win."

An early indication that the financial problems that burdened the Braves last year are continuing into a new season was provided during the collegiate draft. Although the club desperately needs help on the court, new President Norm Sonju traded away the Braves' first-round choice to Chicago for $150,000 and the Bulls' second-round pick.

Sonju explained this debatable move by saying he was hoping to draft the colorful Cedric "Cornbread" Maxwell of UNC-Charlotte, but once Maxwell was picked by Boston, Sonju made the deal with Chicago.

So the best the Braves could do in the draft was Kentucky guard Larry Johnson, the 24th pick overall. General Manager Bob MacKinnon called Johnson "an excellent defensive player who penetrates well. We expect him to be a contender for a starting guard position."

Earlier that same week, Buffalo had dealt away its other first-round pick, the third overall, to Milwaukee for veteran center Swen Nater, who averaged 12 rebounds a game last season to rank seventh in the league. To MacKinnon, "he is the type of center around which an offense can be built."

In another transaction that may be of little consequence, Buffalo obtained guard Johnny Neumann from Los Angeles. Neumann, once a college hotshot, averaged six points a game last season.

With all the dark clouds hanging over Buffalo, some light did manage to shine through, primarily in the person of small forward Adrian Dantley, the NBA's Rookie of the Year, and veteran guard Randy Smith, who asserted himself as the team leader. They were the only consistent scorers on the Braves, with Smith averaging 20.7 points and Dantley 20.3.

Smith, who hinted strongly that he too wanted to leave Buffalo until he was satisfied at the end of the campaign with a lucrative two-year contract, is the second leading scorer in team history (behind McAdoo) with 8444 points—a 17.4 average—and holds six other club records. The 6-3 New York native led all guards in the NBA in rebounding last season with 457, was 10th in steals with 176, and was 11th in assists with 441.

Before signing, Smith had talked of all the trouble on the Braves, saying, "We had turmoil, our team folded on offense and defense with all the changes in personnel. We haven't been playing well and we were all discouraged at not getting into the playoffs."

But after making the biggest score of his life at the negotiating table, the speedy guard said he was looking forward "to a new era. I think the Braves have a great future here in Buffalo and all we need are a couple of players and I think we can be a contender again."

Never mind the future. The Braves might not be having a present if it weren't for Dantley, who provided Buffalo fans with some excuse for buying tickets to Memorial Auditorium. His baptism came under fire, since he was replacing Jim McMillian, the popular team captain who had been sold to the Knicks. But as Dantley recalled, "As soon as I got 15 points and 19 rebounds, the people were on my side."

He neglected to mention it, but that breakthrough came in the season opener against Milwaukee.

A former Notre Dame star who played on the winning American team in the Montreal Olympics, Dantley was only the sixth pick in the 1976 draft. "They said I was too small for a forward and too big and slow for a guard in this league," said the 6-5, 210-pounder. "I would have been the first player picked if I was 6-7. But they were looking at inches, not the player."

With his 20.3 average, Dantley broke the club's rookie scoring record set four years earlier by McAdoo, and with 251 offensive rebounds he ranked second in the NBA in that category among small forwards.

Another record setter was peppery guard Ernie DiGregorio, who smashed an 18-year-old NBA standard with a .945 foul shooting percentage. Ernie D, reinstated to the starting lineup after Tates Locke was fired as coach in January, hit his last 30 free throw attempts in winning the NBA title for the second time in four years, although he only averaged 10.7 points a game.

Center George Johnson, acquired in mid-season from Golden State, provided strong defensive help and ranked sixth in the NBA in blocked shots with 177. According to MacKinnon, who served as interim coach between Locke and Joe Mullaney, "He's given our club a defensive dimension that we've never had before. He's a veteran and a real intelligent person and it's good for our younger players to have someone like him around."

But Johnson averaged only six points a game, and aside from Smith, Dantley and DiGregorio, only John Shumate, at 15.1, averaged in double figures.

Coming off such a frustrating campaign, the Braves desperately needed an infusion of new talent. Instead, despite the fact they could have had two first-round selections, they experienced the least productive draft of their existence.

It should be another cold winter in Buffalo.

PREDICTION: FOURTH

Player's name — Statistics for 1976-77 season

Career statistics, not including those of the 1976-77 season

Player's name (Years in NBA prior to 1976-77)	G	M	FGM	FTM	PTS	AVG	FG%	REB	ASST
Adams, Don (6 years)	77	1710	216	129	561	7.3	.411	371	150
Averitt, Bird (3 years)	410	10,697	1466	743	3675	9.0	.401	2361	719
†(3 years)	75	1136	234	121	589	7.9	.378	78	134
Dantley, Adrian	236	5942	1311	671	3349	14.2	.422	519	748
	77	2816	544	476	1564	20.3	.520	587	144
DiGregorio, Ernie (3 years)	81	2267	365	138	868	10.7	.417	184	378
Foster, Fred	179	4986	815	295	1925	10.8	.414	376	1079
(7 years)	59	689	99	30	228	3.9	.401	76	48
*Gerard, Gus	464	8427	1602	661	3865	8.3	.415	1199	553
†(2 years)	65	1048	201	78	480	7.4	.443	217	92
**Gianelli, John	166	4429	886	381	2158	13.0	.441	1868	530
(4 years)	76	1913	257	90	604	7.9	.444	475	83
***Johnson, George	284	7068	955	364	2274	8.0	.472	1734	380
(4 years)	78	1652	198	71	467	6.0	.462	611	104
§Nater, Swen	286	4824	531	196	1258	4.4	.475	1861	230
†(3 years)	72	1960	383	172	938	13.0	.528	865	108
****Neumann, Johnny	233	6878	1282	473	3037	13.0	.533	3043	281
†(5 years)	63	937	161	59	381	6.0	.406	72	141
Shumate, John	372	9332	2211	991	5558	14.9	.455	1148	1167
(1 year)	74	2601	407	302	1116	15.1	.502	701	159
Smith, Randy	75	1976	332	212	876	11.7	.561	554	127
(5 years)	82	3094	702	294	1698	20.7	.467	457	441
	404	13,610	2786	1174	6746	16.7	.479	1835	2012

BUFFALO BRAVES

	G	M	FGM	FTM	PTS	AVG	FG%	REB	ASST
*Williams, Chuck	65	867	78	68	224	3.4	.371	101	132
†(6 years)	500	15,025	2239	1646	6140	12.3	.473	1251	2420

*—Combined Denver-Buffalo totals
***—Combined Knicks-Buffalo totals
****—Combined Golden State-Buffalo totals
$—Acquired from Milwaukee
****—Combined Buffalo-Los Angeles totals
†—ABA totals

Most Promising Rookies: Larry Johnson. The Braves had the Rookie of the Year last season in Adrian Dantley, but the new crop of rookies probably is the weakest in club history. After trading away two first-round picks, Buffalo didn't make a selection until 24th place overall, then didn't choose again until the fourth round. Johnson, a 6-3, 185-pound guard from Kentucky, has a fine chance to make the team, although he won't make the impression that Dantley did.

PERFORMANCE QUOTIENTS

Offense: After trading away such people as Bob McAdoo, Moses Malone and Tom McMillen, there wasn't that much left. As a result, the Braves, who had ranked second in offense the previous two years, dropped to the middle of the pack with a 105 point per game average. With McAdoo gone, Smith and Dantley took over the scoring burden, averaging 20.7 and 20.3 points, respectively. Dantley, saying he'll do better with experience, nevertheless broke McAdoo's team rookie scoring mark. Shumate, whose pro career got off to a spotty start, showed strong potential by playing in 74 games and averaging 15.1 points, 3.5 points better than he achieved as a rookie. DiGregorio was the only other Brave to reach double figures, hitting 10.7. **Perf. Qt.: 3.**

Defense: For the third consecutive year, the Braves found themselves ranking as the fourth worst defensive team in the NBA, and their yield of 109.5 points was three points a game higher than in 1975-76. Again, the Braves were hurt here by the absence of McAdoo. Johnson, acquired from Golden State in mid-season, provided valuable defensive help, ranking sixth in the league in blocked shots with 177. **Perf. Qt.: 4.**

Rebounding: With McAdoo, the big man gone, Shumate took over the club rebounding leadership with 701, while Johnson compiled 611. More help can be anticipated with the arrival of Nater, who ranked seventh in the NBA last season with 865 rebounds. There would seem to be good balance here as Smith led all guards in the league last season with 457 rebounds, while Dantley grabbed 587. **Perf. Qt.: 3.**

Atlantic Division

New Jersey Nets

Prediction: Fifth

Champagne, magnums of it, bubbly all over the floor, a fine spray jetting through the air, shouts of childlike joy, thoughtful expressions of satisfaction, congratulations on a job well done . . . this is how the New York Nets concluded their American Basketball Association existence.

The conclusion to their first season in the National Basketball Association was more like escaping town on a bus in the dead of night with $1.59 in their pockets, a pint of cheap wine in a paper bag and a dry cheese sandwich.

Indeed, they wound up sneaking out of town, albeit in the light of summer, deserting their home on Long Island for New Jersey. They will play the next two years in the Rutgers gym at Piscataway before moving into a permanent arena to be built for them in the Meadowlands Sports Complex.

The New York Nets quite simply were champions in 1976 and the question of which league they ruled did not diminish their accomplishment the slightest bit. One year later, they were losers. There were sufficient reasons, but they were losers all the same.

The New York Nets owed their championship to

one man. Then they went through season-long humiliation because of the same man—Julius Erving.

The astounding Dr. J brought the Nets a championship in 1976, then left the Nets for dead in 1977. Without Erving, the Nets were merely a run-of-the-mill ball club—on their best night. On their worst, and it would be difficult to single out one of the many, they were an embarrassment not only to themselves but to the NBA as well.

Nets Coach Kevin Loughery was offered the Washington Bullets' job during the off-season, but turned it down to remain with the Nets, not aware of the frustration and disappointment in store.

But, during the summer, Loughery had a lot of reasons to be optimistic. In Erving he had a player capable of assuring the Nets a respectable showing in their first NBA season.

Then, before the season began, the Nets got All-Star guard Nate "Tiny" Archibald from the Kansas City Kings in exchange for Brian Taylor and Jim Eakins. Things could not look any better for the Nets. The combination of Erving and Archibald gave the Nets a good shot at the playoffs and guaranteed they would have the most exciting team in the league. No one suspected the blockbuster trade was going to be responsible for destroying the Nets.

Erving claimed Nets owner Roy Boe had promised to renegotiate his contract if the ABA and NBA ever merged, and the superstar forward grew quite adamant in his demand for a new contract after Archibald became the highest paid player on the Nets.

Boe, who consistently has lost money on the Nets and was paying a large fortune as part of the merger agreement, was equally adamant there would be no new contract, so Erving refused to report to training camp.

Consequently, the Nets boarded a plane bound for their NBA debut in Oakland against the Warriors without Erving. And, when the plane landed, they were informed that Philadelphia 76ers owner F. Eugene Dixon had purchased Erving for $3-million.

"How could anyone do this to us?" Nets guard John Williamson wondered aloud. "Our season is over already."

But the team pulled itself together to spring a 104-103 upset in their first game. It was characteristic of the way this team kept trying, despite a steady succession of misfortune.

Archibald and Williamson proved they could not play in the same backcourt, not getting along at all, but it became a moot point when Archibald was sidelined for the remainder of the season with a broken foot. He had lasted only 34 games, with a scoring average of 20.5.

Rich Jones, a starter on the Nets' championship squad, also lasted only 34 games, being waived into involuntary retirement.

A thoroughly disenchanted Williamson had made it clear he was playing out his option with no chance of his returning to the Nets. So, after 42 games, Williamson was traded to the Indiana Pacers for a first-round draft choice and a player to be named at the conclusion of the season. The player turned out to be Darnell Hillman.

With Williamson's departure, the only starter left from the Nets' championship squad was Kim Hughes, who had shared the center position with Eakins. He averaged only 4.0 points last season as the starter.

The Nets were left with only one player capable of

putting the ball through the hoop with any degree of consistency, a guy named Bubbles Hawkins who had been unemployed through the first two months of the campaign.

The 6-foot-4 Hawkins had been released by the Warriors at the beginning of the season and was ready to embark on a career as a summons server in Detroit before he was signed by the Nets December 15. After Archibald broke his foot and Williamson was traded, Hawkins got his chance to establish himself in the NBA.

Hawkins, equally satisfied to shoot over his opponents or to drive by them to the basket, averaged 19.3 points a game and had a high game of 44 points.

Hawkins finally got some offensive support from forward Mike Bantom, who averaged 18.6 points a game in the final 33 games of the season after being obtained from Seattle.

Hillman, known as Dr. Dunk, won't make Nets' fans forget Dr. J, but he can be just as exciting when he struts his stuff shot. The six-year veteran led the Pacers with 693 rebounds last year, only two fewer than Erving had with Philadelphia. And although he's no match for Julius as an outside shooter or ball-handler, he did shoot 44.3 per cent in averaging 10.7 points a game.

Although he's been primarily a forward, Hillman may be called upon to spell Hughes at center, or may even beat him out for the starting job.

The Nets used their only high draft choice to select forward Bernard King from Tennessee. King, who went hardship after his junior year, had a 25.8 scoring average. Although King's defense is suspect, the Nets' greatest need is scoring.

PREDICTION: FIFTH

Statistics for 1976-77 season

Career statistics, not including those of the 1976-77 season

Player's name / Years in NBA prior to 1976-77	G	M	FGM	FTM	PTS	AVG	FG%	REB	ASST
Archibald, Nate (6 years)	34	1277	250	197	697	20.5	.446	80	254
*Bantom, Mike (3 years)	433	17,520	3946	3002	10,894	25.2	.467	1207	3499
Bassett, Tim (3 years)	77	1909	361	224	946	12.3	.478	476	102
†(3 years)	231	5792	952	462	2366	10.2	.439	1436	427
	76	2442	293	101	687	9.0	.396	641	109
**Davis, Mel (3 years)	238	5642	650	239	1543	6.5	.286	1652	291
Fox, Jim (9 years)	56	1094	168	64	400	7.1	.362	293	71
	134	1478	263	82	608	4.5	.385	523	93
	71	1165	184	95	463	6.5	.462	329	49
Hawkins, Bubbles (1 year)	672	16,129	2427	1628	6482	9.6	.480	5196	1152
	52	1481	406	194	1006	19.3	.447	154	93
	32	153	53	20	126	3.9	.510	97	16
***Hillman, Darnell (5 years)	82	2302	359	161	879	10.7	.443	693	166
Hughes, Kim (1 year)	395	11,015	1717	756	4195	10.6	.486	3306	551
	81	2081	151	19	321	4.0	.427	564	98
Skinner, Al (2 years)	84	2162	300	92	692	8.2	.530	775	55
Terry, Chuck (2 years)	79	2256	382	231	996	12.6	.431	363	289
	134	2855	460	275	1198	8.9	.451	427	401
	61	1075	128	48	304	5.0	.403	143	39
van Breda Kolff, Jan (2 years)	74	725	59	17	135	1.8	.339	148	1
	72	2398	271	195	737	10.2	.445	460	117
†(2 years)	164	3617	378	342	1100	6.7	.460	794	363

NEW JERSEY NETS

	G	M	FGM	FTM	PTS	AVG	FG%	REB	ASST
****Wohl, Dave (5 years)	51	986	116	61	293	5.7	.400	81	142
	349	7038	887	451	2225	6.4	.435	473	1242

*—Combined Seattle-N.Y. Nets totals
**—Combined N.Y. Knicks-N.Y. Nets totals
***—Acquired from Indiana
****—Combined Houston-N.Y. Nets totals
†—ABA totals

Most Promising Rookies: Bernard King, Robert Elmore. King definitely will find a place on the Nets, who are desperately in need of someone who can score. The second half of last season Hawkins and Bantom were their only scoring threats. Scoring is one thing King can provide. He averaged 25.8 points a game for Tennessee last season. Defensively, though, King was not such a standout. Elmore, younger brother of Indiana center Len Elmore, was the third leading rebounder in the nation last season with an average of 15.8 for Wichita State. Offensively, though, he is not much of a threat.

PERFORMANCE QUOTIENTS

Offense: The Nets were the lowest scoring team in the NBA last season, but there could be some dramatic improvement this season with a healthy Archibald and the addition of Bernard King. Archibald has led the league in scoring, so he can make a big difference. Also, when he was playing last season, Archibald did not get along with his backcourt partner, John Williamson, who was traded to Indiana. If Archibald and Hawkins can get along, the Nets will have one of the highest scoring backcourts in the league. Archibald averaged 20.5 points a game last season and Hawkins 19.3. Bantom, who came to the Nets from Seattle last season, averaged 18.6 points for his 33 games with New York. But he was the Nets' only scorer on the front line. Hillman averaged 10.7 points a game for Indiana and certainly will provide more scoring from the center position than Hughes. **Perf. Qt.: 4.**

Defense: This was the Nets' saving grace last season and the only reason they won 22 games. However, one reason only two teams in the league allowed fewer points was that the Nets played a slowdown offense, keeping their games low scoring. However, with increased scoring potential, Coach Loughery probably will try to get a fast break offense going, which will take its toll defensively. **Perf. Qt.: 3.**

Rebounding: The Nets are extremely weak in this department with Bassett and Hughes their two best. Hillman, a super leaper, will be a big help here. **Perf. Qt.: 4.**

Central Division

Washington Bullets

Prediction: First

However often they change their home, their name and their personnel, the Washington Bullets are unable to escape their destiny.

In the seven years since 1970, during which time the franchise has been known as Baltimore, Capital and finally Washington, the Bullets have been consistently aggravating, persistently frustrating and seemingly trapped on a treadmill.

Five years in a row they won the Central Division title, and the last two years they finished one game out with identical records of 48-34. Perennial powers during regular season play, they seem to do a complete turnabout when the big money is on the line.

In the last nine years, the Bullets have been eliminated seven times in the first full playoff round, such as they were last spring by the upstart Houston Rockets. The other two years they advanced to the finals, but on both occasions were wiped out in four-game sweeps.

As Dick Motta begins his second full year as head coach, he isn't concerned about the past. In fact, pointing to the rebuilding job that he started, he wasn't all that disappointed.

"We finished with the fifth best record in the league,"

he pointed out, "and I'm looking forward to this new year. We'll be much more organized and we'll be better."

General Manager Bob Ferry, who has been around the Bullet scene a lot longer, also looked to the bright side. "To analyze wins and losses is only relative to the competition, and the competition in the league was as tough as it's been in nine years."

If, though, the Bullets continue to tread time on the same beaten trail, it will be with a new cast of players. Oh, familiar names such as Elvin Hayes, Phil Chenier, Wes Unseld and Dave Bing are still available, and Chenier and Hayes figure to play important roles. But this is now the team of Mitch Kupchak, Larry Wright, Tom Henderson, Kevin Grevey, Greg Ballard and Bo Ellis.

"We can build with this team," Ferry said. "We have to decide which position to commit to Mitch, big forward or center, and then kind of build around him. But he's flexible enough to make that an easy thing to do."

The 6-9 Kupchak and Wright, a 6-1 guard, both were plucked on the first round of the 1976 draft, and the Bullets again had two first-round choices last spring. With the No. 4 pick overall, they took Ballard, a 6-7, 215-pound forward from Oregon, and then selected Ellis, a 6-9, 200-pound forward from Marquette.

Of Ballard, who averaged 21.7 points last season, hitting 53 per cent of his shots, with almost 10 rebounds a game, Motta gloated, "His great strength is that he doesn't have any weaknesses. He's probably as good a passer as there is among the major college players. When we use Mitch more and more at forward, we will need his rebounding help. He's ready to play NBA defense right now. I don't think you could go through a more regimented and tougher physical program than at Oregon."

Ellis averaged 15.6 points in helping Marquette to the NCAA championship, and Hank Raymonds, moving up to succeed Al McGuire as the Warriors' head coach, called him "the most intelligent player I've handled in my 13 years here. He's also the most unselfish ball player."

Guard Phil Walker of Millersville (Pa.) State, the team's second round pick, also was given a good shot at making the squad, as was another guard, Coniel Norman, signed as a free agent after having played two years with Philadelphia.

Thus, Ferry visualized his depth chart as such: "At shooting guard we've got Phil Chenier and Coniel Norman. At playmaker we've got Tom Henderson and Larry Wright. At center we've got Unseld and Kupchak. At small forward we've got Kevin Grevey and Ballard. We needed someone to back up Hayes [which would be Ellis], and I can also see Bo on the floor with Elvin and a center."

Although he handled the "sixth man" role as a rookie, filling in at center and forward, Kupchak very well might be the most important player on the Washington roster. As Ferry said, "Every time a team talks trade with us, they mention Mitch." After Truck Robinson was dealt to Atlanta for Henderson, Kupchak frequently filled in at small forward behind Grevey.

"I feel very comfortable with Mitch in there," Motta said. "He can run with anybody and he really hustles the boards. He's so big, he's always got a mismatch because the other team has to play its big forward against Hayes."

Kupchak, who played center on the champion U.S. Olympic team at Montreal, appeared in all 82 games for Washington, averaging 10.4 points in his limited time with 494 rebounds. However, he placed second to Kareem Abdul-Jabbar in field goal percentage at .572.

Wright, who passed up his last year at Grambling to join the pros, got more time than anticipated because of a knee injury to Jimmy Jones. Playing for the most part behind Chenier and Bing, the speedy, confident guard proved himself a take-charge guy as he averaged 7.8 points and added 232 assists.

Hayes and Unseld, who have been the backbone of the Bullets for the past six years, both expressed a desire to be traded, but this is less likely to occur in the case of Hayes. A nine-time All-Star, Hayes had another superb season, leading the NBA in minutes played (3364) and the Bullets in scoring (23.7), rebounding (1029) and blocked shots (220). The 6-9 forward blamed criticism of his play and relations with teammates for his request.

"It bothers me and hurts me that people don't think I did enough," Hayes said. "Kareem [Abdul-Jabbar] is the only player who has done more. I don't think there are five players in the league who could match my stats and I'm not asked to do just one thing. I could lead the league in scoring, rebounding or blocked shots and I play good defense. But the thing is that I have to do all those things."

Unseld, although playing a full schedule for the first time in seven years, averaged 7.8 points and 877 rebounds, his poorest output as a pro except for 1973-74, when injuries limited him to 56 games.

Chenier, an excellent one-on-one player and a streaky shooter, was second in club scoring with a 20.2 average while Henderson averaged 11.2 and placed fifth in the NBA in assists with 598.

PREDICTION: FIRST

Player's name — Statistics for 1976-77 season

Career statistics, not including those of the 1976-77 season

Years in NBA prior to 1976-77	G	M	FGM	FTM	PTS	AVG	FG%	REB	ASST
Bing, Dave (10 years)	64	1516	271	136	678	10.6	.454	143	275
Chenier, Phil (5 years)	757	28,997	6269	4023	16,561	21.9	.440	3065	4822
	78	2842	654	270	1578	20.2	.444	299	294
	385	14,020	3050	1233	7333	19.0	.448	1556	1248
*Gray, Leonard (2 years)	83	1639	258	118	634	7.6	.436	293	124
	141	4419	772	230	1774	12.6	.481	876	366
Grevey, Kevin (1 year)	76	1306	224	79	527	6.9	.423	178	68
	56	504	79	52	210	3.8	.371	60	27
Hayes, Elvin (8 years)	82	3364	760	422	1942	23.7	.501	1029	158
	652	27,843	6414	3092	15,920	24.4	.442	9873	1348
**Henderson, Tom (2 years)	87	2791	371	233	975	11.2	.449	239	598
	160	5031	836	384	2056	12.9	.412	477	688
Kupchak, Mitch	82	1513	341	170	852	10.4	.572	494	62
Pace, Joe	30	119	24	16	64	2.1	.436	34	4
Unseld, Wes (8 years)	82	2860	270	100	640	7.8	.490	877	363
	600	22,917	2944	1345	7233	12.1	.501	9340	2282
Weiss, Bob (2 years)	62	768	62	29	153	2.5	.466	69	130
	721	16,509	2226	1384	5836	8.1	.427	1329	2801
Wright, Larry	78	1421	262	88	612	7.8	.440	98	232

*—Combined Seattle-Washington totals   **—Combined Atlanta-Washington totals

WASHINGTON BULLETS

Most Promising Rookies: Greg Ballard, Bo Ellis, Phil Walker. Ballard, the fourth man chosen in the draft, appears to be the complete player. Performing for a defensive-oriented team at Oregon, the 6-7, 215-pound forward averaged 21.7 points last season with 283 rebounds. According to General Manager Bob Ferry, "Ballard, besides having brute strength, is a very good basketball player in the fundamental phases. He's by far the best player that has made his team a winner. He makes people around him play better." Ellis, described as an intelligent, unselfish player, is a 6-9 forward who averaged 15.6 points on Marquette's NCAA championship team, and Walker, a 6-2 guard, was a 26.7 scorer with 319 rebounds at Millersville State.

PERFORMANCE QUOTIENTS

Offense: With a heavy influx of good, young talent, better days appear ahead for the Bullets. They'll still be depending on the destructive 1-2 punch of Hayes and Chenier to carry the offense, but these two arm-weary veterans will have a stronger supporting cast. Last season Hayes and Chenier accounted for 44 points a game between them, with no one else averaging as much as 12 points. But in the draft Washington took two strong forwards, Greg Ballard and Bo Ellis. Ballard was a 53 per cent shooter at Oregon last season when he averaged 21.7 points and Ellis scored at a 15.6 clip for Marquette. Kupchak, in a part-time role, still averaged 10.4 points with a superb 57 per cent accuracy mark, and Wright, who broke in with a 7.8 average, is capable of bigger production if needed. Henderson, along with an 11.2 average, ranked fifth in the NBA in assists with 598 while Unseld, with the good outlet pass, added 363. After falling under 20 points for the first time in his career in 1975-76, Hayes climbed back into eighth place in the NBA scoring race with a 23.7 average while Chenier was at 20.2. Hayes, saying he no longer forces shots from out of position, also had a .501 shooting percentage, far above his career average of .442. **Perf. Qt.: 2.**

Defense: Coach Dick Motta credits Hayes with doing a tremendous job of clogging up the middle, and the Big E was the third most effective shot blocker in the league with 220, while coming up with 87 steals. Henderson, who had 138 steals, and Wright both are young with good speed, and should provide Washington with a tight backcourt. The name of the game at Oregon is defense, so Ballard is expected to provide immediate help here as well. Chenier contributed 120 steals and Unseld is a defensive-minded player. **Perf. Qt.: 2.**

Rebounding: Thanks to Hayes and Unseld, Washington has been a fairly strong rebounding team through the years, and it should improve this season with the additions of Ballard and Ellis and more playing time for Kupchak. Hayes was sixth in rebounding last season with 1029, the eighth time in nine years he has exceeded 1000, and Unseld added 877. Kupchak, with limited playing time, had 494. **Perf. Qt.: 2.**

Central Division

Houston Rockets

Prediction: Second

It would be too simplistic to say that Moses led the Houston Rockets out of the wilderness. Instead, let it be noted that he was the main man marching to the tempo set by Cool Hand Luke.

Houston, as the record makes ever so clear, enjoyed the best campaign of its history last season with a 49-33 log. This was the fourth best mark in the NBA (only one game behind both Philadelphia and Denver), enabling the Rockets to win their first ever division title, and they advanced as far as the semifinals in the playoffs, once again their best showing.

Let the record show that only two players of consequence were added to the Houston lineup last season, huge, muscular Moses Malone and slick, perceptive John Lucas. Together, they injected the perfect combination of power that finally lifted the Rockets off the launch pad.

Traditionally, the Rockets are one of the better-shooting teams in the league, particularly in the six years they have had Rudy Tomjanovich, Calvin Murphy and Mike Newlin. In Malone, they added the best offensive rebounder in the game, as well as a capable scorer, and in Lucas they acquired a natural leader with an ambition to be president of the United States.

"We've been a good shooting team in the seven years I've been here," Murphy stated. "What we gained last year was defense and boards. We've built around Moses.

"Moses gave us the scoring and rebounding we needed underneath. We already had shooters, a bench and a coach who lets us improvise and take the shots when we feel we have them."

Added Newlin, "Our team is not that much different from the year before, except deeper. It's just that we've added Malone and Lucas."

With a front line that often consisted of 7-foot Kevin Kunnert at center and Malone and Tomjanovich at forward, the Rockets found themselves being compared to water buffaloes. But they could shoot with anyone, and often used the fast break made possible by the board work of Malone, Tomjanovich and Kunnert.

Malone, who once played for Coach Tom Nissalke with the Utah Stars of the ABA, then was acquired early last season by Houston from Buffalo, broke Paul Silas' NBA record for offensive rebounds with 437. In nine games, the 6-11, 23-year-old forward cleared 10 or more offensive rebounds.

"Moses thinks that anything that hits the backboard is his," Murphy said. "He doesn't realize that there are nine other guys on the court."

When Houston eliminated Washington from the playoffs, Bullet Coach Dick Motta said with due respect, "I've never seen a guy control the offensive boards the way he does. Ninety per cent of it is quickness and desire. He really did a job on us."

In one of the games, Malone equaled the NBA season high with 15 offensive rebounds, causing Mitch Kupchak of Washington to remark: "Moses is really something. He gets great position and always seems to be around the ball. He has quick hands, long arms and good jumping ability. He's not a great jumper, but his timing is great. He just seems to slither in front of you."

In addition to his board work, Malone averaged 13.2 points for the season and placed seventh in the league in blocked shots with 181. Unfortunately, it may be a while before his fans can feel closer to the baby giant since he usually doesn't have much to say. Even Nissalke admitted last season, "At first he was very quiet, very suspicious of me. It took us a month, six weeks to start any kind of relationship."

One man who got close to Moses, and helped influence him for the better, was Lucas. The rookie guard helped Malone find an apartment in his building, and then tried to tutor him.

Lucas, the No. 1 pick in the 1976 collegiate draft, gradually replaced Newlin in the starting backcourt alongside Murphy, although all three played in every game and saw a lot of duty. But Newlin, who sometimes was used at small forward, didn't express any public resentment, saying instead, "He inserted himself without infringing on anybody else's space, which is really an art. He could score 40 points a game, but he'd still find a way to credit the team."

Lucas also said he didn't feel resentment from Murphy or Newlin, adding, "Once they found out I wasn't a scoring guard, there wasn't any problem.

"My role is to provide leadership, and I will measure my value to the team by how well we perform as a team. My offense comes out of the flow of the game. I don't come down the floor four or five straight times and go one-on-one. Basketball is a game of quickness rather than size, and I use my quickness to get off my shot."

Murphy, only 5-9, has been called by Nissalke "one of our most consistent players. He's a floor leader and he makes things happen. His quickness creates a lot of problems for the opposition."

Murphy matched his career scoring average of 17.9 last season, led the team in steals with 144, and his 386 assists were second to Lucas' 463.

Newlin, one of the most intelligent players in the league and one who thrives on pressure situations, also averaged in double figures with a 12.7 mark, and Lucas was at 11.1.

Tomjanovich, rarely a threat to drive, still led Houston in scoring again with a 21.6 average and contributed 684 rebounds, and Kunnert, with a 9.4 scoring average and 669 rebounds, was something of a surprise.

"Kevin is getting smarter," Nissalke said late last season. "We're running more things for him and he's learning to use the offense better."

To people like Tomjanovich and Murphy, who had been in the playoffs only once before, last season was a dream.

"You had to be here when we were 1-18 to appreciate winning like this," Murphy said. "There were nights when we used to have to sneak out of the building with our heads down in shame."

Said Tomjanovich after Houston clinched the Central Division title: "This is unbelievable. For me, it's like coming out of a tunnel."

Nissalke, chosen NBA Coach of the Year in his first season with the Rockets, prefers to look ahead.

"Our team has a great history in front of it," he said. "The guys like Rudy, Calvin and Mike will improve in lesser amounts the next few years. But Mo, Luke and Kevin have their careers in front of them."

PREDICTION: SECOND

Player's name — Statistics for 1976-77 season

Years in NBA prior to 1976-77	G	M	FGM	FTM	PTS	AVG	FG%	REB	ASST
Jones, Dwight (3 years)	74	1239	167	101	435	5.9	.494	284	48
Kunnert, Kevin (3 years)	215	5296	812	411	2035	9.5	.452	1675	321
Lucas, John	81	2050	333	93	759	9.4	.486	669	154
	219	4837	916	239	2071	9.5	.496	1635	306
	82	2531	388	135	911	11.1	.477	219	463
*Malone, Moses †(2 years)	82	2506	389	305	1083	13.2	.480	1072	89
	126	4373	842	487	2171	17.2	.553	1622	140
Murphy, Calvin (6 years)	82	2764	596	272	1464	17.9	.490	172	386
	482	14,685	3326	1967	8619	17.9	.481	1222	2564
Newlin, Mike (5 years)	82	2119	387	269	1043	12.7	.455	204	320
	401	12,518	2305	1465	6075	15.1	.462	1426	1767
Owens, Tom †(5 years)	46	462	68	52	188	4.1	.504	142	18
	389	9365	1720	837	4286	11.0	.522	2975	549
Ratleff, Ed (3 years)	37	533	70	26	166	4.5	.435	77	43
	233	6737	960	428	2348	10.1	.461	1124	700
Tomjanovich, Rudy (6 years)	81	3130	733	287	1753	21.6	.510	684	172
	476	15,996	3427	1390	8244	17.3	.503	4238	1042
White, Rudy (1 year)	46	368	47	15	109	2.4	.443	41	35
	32	284	42	18	102	3.2	.412	38	30

*—Combined Buffalo-Houston totals   †—ABA totals

Most Promising Rookies: Larry Moffett, Robert Reid. Although they have good strength up front, the Rockets still went for a pair of forwards with their two second-round picks (they had traded away their first choice). Moffett, 6-9 and 210 pounds, played only 23 minutes a game at Nevada-Las Vegas last season, sharing time at center with Lewis Brown. In his limited service, Moffett averaged eight points a game and 9.2 rebounds. Reid, a 6-8, 205-pounder, averaged 16.4 points and 8.4 rebounds in his final campaign at St. Mary's (Tex.).

PERFORMANCE QUOTIENTS

Offense: Perhaps there is a valuable lesson to be learned from the Rockets. For years they stressed a run 'n' shoot game, and annually ranked among the team leaders in offense. While they still have some sharp gunners, they are now putting the emphasis on an all-around effort, and last season they ranked 12th in the NBA in team offense with a 106.4 average. Yet, they enjoyed the best campaign of their history and advanced as far as the playoff semifinals. Tomjanovich, although slow and with little ability to penetrate with the ball on his own, led Houston scorers with a 21.6 average, the second best figure of his career. Murphy, who has more than enough quickness but at 5-9 not nearly enough size, was next in scoring at 17.9, and he had a .490 field goal percentage, fine for a guard. In fact, the Rockets as a team hit at a .483 clip, the third best mark in the NBA and an indication they haven't lost their shooting touch. With the addition of Malone (13.2) to support Tomjanovich, the Houston attack is more diversified and not so dependent on the guards. Perf. Qt.: 2.

Defense: Any time you have a giant bull such as Malone clogging up the middle, your defense just has to be better for it, and so it was for Houston. After yielding 107 points per game in 1975-76, the Rockets allowed only 104.8 last season, certainly not bad at all for a team that never used to think defense. Malone ranked seventh in the league in blocked shots with 181—and also had 67 steals—while Kunnert proved to be another giant obstacle for rival shooters as he knocked down 105 shots. Before a shot could be fired, Murphy managed 144 steals and Lucas had 125. Perf. Qt.: 2.

Rebounding: In 1975-76, Houston ranked next to last in total rebounds. Then along came Moses. Malone actually cleared more rebounds than anyone in the league last season with 1072, although Portland's Bill Walton won the statistical crown since he played in fewer games. Malone did break the NBA record for offensive rebounds with 437, and he was helped considerably on the boards by Tomjanovich, with 684 total rebounds, and Kunnert, with 669. Houston's two top draft choices, Larry Moffett and Robert Reid, are rebounding forwards. Perf. Qt.: 2.

Central Division

Cleveland Cavaliers

Prediction: Third

Austin Carr finally had a season of perfect health. Unfortunately, the same could not be said of his Cleveland Cavaliers teammates.

While Carr played in all 82 regular-season games and was second in playing time with 2409 minutes, the Cavaliers were struck by several key injuries, the most damaging the one to 35-year-old center Nate Thurmond.

Consequently, after the best start in the National Basketball Association, the Cavaliers barely qualified for the playoffs with a 43-39 record and were eliminated in the first round by the Washington Bullets.

During one stretch of the season, Cleveland had its leading scorer, Campy Russell; its ball-handling guard, Jim Cleamons, and Thurmond all sidelined with injuries.

After winning the Central Division title the previous season, it had to be a disappointing year for the Cavs.

Ironically, though, it concluded with Coach Bill Fitch being given a new multiple-year contract.

It's ironic because after the 1975-76 season, the most successful in the history of the Cleveland franchise, Fitch and Cavaliers owner Nick Mileti were at war with each other in the press. An uneasy truce was reached and Fitch returned to the Cavaliers last season and adversity apparently forged a new bond between the two.

In announcing the new contract, Mileti credited Fitch with helping to build "one of the premier franchises in our league. We look forward to fulfilling our goal of an NBA championship."

Fitch has been the Cavaliers' coach since their inception in 1970 and is the only coach from that expansion class still in the NBA. His career record is 231-343.

Last season, though, certainly had to be the most frustrating of Fitch's career. The Cavaliers won their first eight games en route to a 16-4 start, but then injuries took their toll.

"I'm playing tired bodies and I've tried never to do that," Fitch said late last season. "We're missing three players and two others are hurt and shouldn't be playing.

"It's a real credit to these guys that they're still hustling and winning. We've done more improvising this season than ever. It's a different lineup every night, but the guys have hung together well and reacted very well to adversity."

Carr, Jim Chones and Dick Snyder were the only three Cavaliers to play in every game.

"It's been a crazy year," said Carr, who averaged 16.2 points a game. "It's like training camp never ended. At a time when we need stability, we're still experimenting.

"I've had to take charge more this season, playing with so many different guys. In the past, Cleamons handled the ball and called the plays, but now I'm doing a lot of that. It really depends on whom I'm playing with as to what my role is. When Foots Walker is in, we run more and he handles the ball. But, when Gary Brokaw is playing, we try to set up more and I call the plays.

"My defensive assignments have changed, too. Cleamons always took the other team's scoring guard, but I've been doing that a lot now because I'm bigger than Foots or Gary.

"It's been quite a year, but in a way it's been helpful because I'm playing more aspects of the game."

Carr, who is the Cavaliers' all-time leading scorer, had 220 assists in contrast to his two previous seasons' totals of 122 and 154.

In mid-season the Cavaliers traded Rowland Garrett and two high draft choices to Milwaukee for Brokaw and 7-foot center Elmore Smith.

The addition of Smith gave the Cavaliers three centers with Thurmond and Chones already on the roster. It seemed an unnecessary surplus, but then Thurmond was injured. For a team whose fortunes hinge on its defensive play, the loss of Thurmond was a major one.

The Cavaliers were second to the Chicago Bulls in points allowed for the second straight season, but scored more than only the Bulls and the New York Nets.

Elmore Smith averaged 8.7 points a game for the Cavs and was the only Cleveland player to rank among the league's top 10 in any category as he finished 10th in blocked shots with an average of 2.06. Brokaw had a scoring average of 7.2 with the Cavaliers.

One of the Cavaliers' many experiments was shifting Chones to forward to get him in the lineup at the same time as Elmore Smith. Chones averaged 12.9 points and more than eight rebounds a game.

Russell, the Cavaliers' small forward, led the team

in scoring with a 16.5 average and Jim Brewer, the big forward, led the team with 762 rebounds. Sixth man Bingo Smith averaged 14.5 points a game and Snyder 9.3.

The Cavaliers' top two draft choices were guards Ed Jordan from Rutgers and Steve Grote from Michigan. Both played in the shadow of more heralded backcourt mates in college, Mike Dabney at Rutgers and Rickey Green at Michigan.

Jordan is a skilled ball-handler with an excellent outside shot, while the sturdily built Grote is known for his aggressive defense.

It was a bit surprising the Cavaliers made guards their top choices because they already seem overloaded in that department. Cleveland did the same thing last year when it selected Kansas State's Chuckie Williams and Maryland's Mo Howard. Williams was hurt and played only 65 minutes last season, and Howard was waived before catching on with the New Orleans Jazz.

Their outstanding defense assures the Cavaliers of a good shot at a playoff berth. And, offensively, they play intelligently, always giving the ball up to the open man. However, the lack of a top scoring threat is a severe limitation the Cavaliers can overcome only partially with their well-disciplined play.

The Cavs have not made any significant additions other than Thurmond since their rise to respectability a few years ago. They can go only so far with their smart play before their lack of talent proves an insurmountable handicap.

PREDICTION: THIRD

Player's name — Statistics for 1976-77 season

Years in NBA prior to 1976-77	G	M	FGM	FTM	PTS	AVG	FG%	REB	ASST
Brewer, Jim (3 years)	81	2672	296	97	689	8.5	.451	767	195
*Brokaw, Gary (2 years)	246	6766	901	323	2125	8.6	.437	1924	486
Carr, Austin (5 years)	80	1487	242	163	647	8.1	.429	123	228
Chones, Jim (2 years)	148	3107	471	285	1227	8.3	.456	272	467
Cleamons, Jim (5 years)	82	2409	558	213	1329	16.2	.457	240	220
Lambert, John (1 year)	311	10,099	2359	904	5622	18.1	.444	1047	1008
Russell, Campy (2 years)	82	2378	450	155	1055	12.9	.463	688	104
Smith, Bobby (7 years)	154	5168	1009	324	2342	15.2	.464	1416	295
*Smith, Elmore (5 years)	60	2045	257	112	626	10.4	.434	273	308
Snyder, Dick (10 years)	355	8761	1245	514	3004	8.5	.457	1119	1276
Thurmond, Nate (13 years)	63	555	67	25	159	2.5	.427	154	31
Walker, Foots (2 years)	54	333	49	25	123	2.3	.445	102	16
	70	2109	435	288	1158	16.5	.434	419	189
	150	2715	633	390	1656	11.0	.463	497	152
	81	2135	513	148	1174	14.5	.446	317	152
	552	14,918	3148	868	7164	13.0	.451	2641	1270
	70	1464	241	117	599	8.6	.475	439	43
	387	14,087	2457	863	5777	14.9	.479	4739	695
	82	1685	316	127	759	9.3	.456	149	160
	768	22,795	4381	1749	10,511	13.7	.493	2486	2488
	49	997	100	68	268	5.5	.407	374	83
	915	34,878	5421	3327	14,169	15.5	.422	14,090	2492
	62	1216	157	89	403	6.5	.450	160	254
	153	2350	254	164	672	4.4	.394	328	480

*—Combined Milwaukee-Cleveland totals

CLEVELAND CAVALIERS

Most Promising Rookies: Ed Jordan, Steve Grote. Jordan is an extremely quick, smooth guard. In leading the potent Rutgers attack the past few years, Jordan has proved an excellent ball-handler and a good outside shot. He also has shown the desire necessary to play good defense. Grote is a well-built, bruising defensive specialist, who played in the Michigan backcourt opposite Rickey Green. He never scored much for the Wolverines, but at times showed a fair touch from the outside. Both will have a tough time making the Cavs' roster as it already seems overloaded with good guards.

PERFORMANCE QUOTIENTS

Offense: The Cavs must rely on their guards for scoring, not the surest way for any team to score points. Forward Russell is the team's leading scorer, but even he relies on outside jumpers. Chones is the only inside scoring threat. He consistently scores around his 13-point average, but rarely has a big game. Last season his highest scoring performance was only 24 points. Russell averaged 16.5 points a game and Bingo Smith 14.5. The Cavaliers are an unselfish lot and would be a great offensive team if they had just one superstar scorer. The closest one to that is guard Carr, who averaged 16.2 points a game. Cleamons had a 10.4 average and Snyder a 9.3. It appears the only team the Cavaliers may outscore this season is the New York Nets. **Perf. Qt.: 4.**

Only the Chicago Bulls allowed fewer points. Center Thurmond is the physical and spiritual leader of the Cleveland defense, but they did well even during his long absence last season. The Cavs play a well-coached team defense in which they continually help out each other. Brewer teams with Thurmond or Chones on the front line to close off the area near the basket and Cleamons leads the Cavs' squad of fleet, aggressive guards. **Perf. Qt.: 1.**

Rebounding: Brewer led the Cavs in rebounding with 762, while Chones had 688. With Elmore Smith and Thurmond, the Cavaliers have the depth and size to hold their own under the backboards. Russell also can be a surprising nuisance under the boards for opponents, grabbing 419 rebounds last season. **Perf. Qt.: 3.**

Defense: This is the area in which the Cavaliers excel.

Central Division

New Orleans Jazz

Prediction: Fourth

Pete Maravich took 360 more shots than anyone else in the National Basketball Association. And, yet, no one could accuse Pistol Pete of being a gun.

One reason is Maravich sank 888 of his 2047 shots from the floor, a .433 percentage, to lead the NBA in scoring with a 31.1 average. The second, and more important reason, is Maravich was the Jazz' only scoring threat.

The Jazz believed they had obtained substantial offensive support for Maravich when they signed guard Gail Goodrich after he played out his option with the Los Angeles Lakers. But the 34-year-old lefthander suffered from a seriously inflamed Achilles tendon and played only 27 games and averaged 12.6 points before missing the rest of the season as the result of surgery.

Goodrich was not the only one to miss a considerable amount of playing time, though. Aaron James missed 30 games, Ron Behagen 22 and Fred Boyd 35.

The Jazz had hoped to make the playoffs last season after compiling the best record of their existence, 38-44, the previous season.

Instead, the Jazz regressed to a 37-45 record.

Worse, they may have lost their second (to Maravich) most important asset. Coach Bill van Breda Kolff, who had guided the Jazz to their surprising 38-44 record, was fired early in the season after a dispute with the front office.

Van Breda Kolff had the Jazz playing .500 ball when a dispute with the front office arose over rookie guard Andy Walker. The front office wanted Walker waived; van Breda Kolff did not. In the end, Walker was cut and so was van Breda Kolff.

Assistant coach Elgin Baylor was named to replace van Breda Kolff. And, ironically, when an injury opened a spot on the roster a week later, the replacement was a guy named Andy Walker.

And who are these geniuses in the Jazz front office? These are the same guys who traded a basketful of top draft picks for Maravich, dooming the Jazz to become a team of one superstar surrounded by a group of nonentities. This trade with Atlanta caused Cotton Fitzsimmons, then the Hawks' coach, to call it "the biggest steal since the Louisiana Purchase."

These are the guys who spent a fortune and more valuable draft picks for Goodrich, who was ailing when he joined the Jazz. And, then, after van Breda Kolff had done so much with so little they had the gall to question his basketball judgment and the stupidity to fire him.

But there was good news for Jazz fans at the end of the season—a long overdue shakeup in the front office.

The Jazz made another attempt to become a playoff contender during the off-season by signing free agent forward Len Robinson. Robinson, obtained by Atlanta from Washington during the season for Tom Henderson, averaged 22.4 points and 10.2 rebounds a game for the Hawks. Robinson is a much greater scoring threat than any of the other forwards on the Jazz and his nickname, "Truck," indicates the kind of muscle he can throw around under the backboards.

In the draft, the Jazz didn't have a pick until the second round and they made St. Bonaventure's Essie Hollis the 44th selection of the draft. The slender 6-6 forward, an extremely fluid player, averaged 21.8 points a game as a senior and helped lead the Bonnies to the National Invitation Tournament championship.

The Jazz' second pick was 6-4 Connecticut swingman Tony Hanson, the nation's 10th leading scorer with a 26-point average.

It was New Orleans' seventh-round choice, though, which attracted the most attention—Lusia Harris, the 6-3 forward who led Delta State to the women's national championship.

It's questionable, though, whether the Jazz have improved themselves enough to make the playoffs. And almost certainly they will not be in the running for the championship which has become such an obsession with Maravich.

"I think some people are destined to become losers and some people are destined to become winners," Maravich said. "Sometimes I feel that maybe I'm destined never to win an NBA championship."

Maravich became the first guard to lead the NBA in scoring since Nate Archibald in 1972-73 and the fifth overall. The others were the Chicago Stags' Max Zaslofsky in 1947-48, the Detroit Pistons' Dave Bing in 1967-68 and Los Angeles' Jerry West in 1969-70. Maravich also became the fourth guard to average more than 30 points a game in a season, the others being Oscar Robertson (six times), West (five times) and Archibald (once). The highlight of Maravich's season was a 68-point performance against the New York Knicks.

But Maravich says, "I've done many personal things in basketball and it really hasn't gotten me what I wanted out of life. The one thing I want more than anything now is to be part of a championship team.

"The championship thing has been walked over and walked over so many times that it gets boring, even to myself, but that's really the only thing I have left to think about in basketball."

This kind of talk had to send shivers through the New Orleans front office because Maravich's contract expired at the conclusion of last season.

That's why their signing Robinson had been so important to them, as a sign of faith to Maravich that they seriously were seeking to become a championship team.

"I have to rely on management's integrity," Maravich had said. "I have to rely on their honesty in wanting to make this franchise a winner in the NBA."

The bumbling in the Jazz' front office has not escaped Maravich's attention.

"The only way you can have a winner is if your management, your players, your trainers, on down to your lowest guy, are in it for one thing—that is to make a success of the franchise," Maravich said.

"There can't be any jealousy among owners. You can't have that at all. The only way you can have a truly great franchise is if everybody's out front."

The addition of Robinson was a step in the right direction, but the Jazz still are a long way from being a championship contender.

NBA EAST: MVPs and All-Stars

John Drew
Atlanta Hawks

NBA EAST: MVPs

Dave Cowens
Boston Celtics

Randy Smith
Buffalo Braves

NBA EAST: MVPs

Austin Carr
Cleveland Cavaliers

Rudy Tomjanovich
Houston Rockets

NBA EAST: MVPs

Pete Maravich
New Orleans Jazz

Bubbles Hawkins
New Jersey Nets

NBA EAST: MVPs

Earl Monroe
New York Knicks

Doug Collins
Philadelphia 76ers

NBA EAST: MVPs

George Gervin
San Antonio Spurs

Elvin Hayes
Washington Bullets

NBA EAST: All-Stars

Julius Erving
Forward
Philadelphia 76ers

Bob McAdoo
Forward
New York Knicks

NBA EAST: All-Stars

Dave Cowens
Center
Boston Celtics

Pete Maravich
Guard
New Orleans Jazz

NBA EAST: All-Stars

Doug Collins
Guard
Philadelphia 76ers

PREDICTION: FOURTH

Statistics for 1976-77 season

Career statistics, not including those of the 1976-77 season

Player's name / Years in NBA prior to 1976-77	G	M	FGM	FTM	PTS	AVG	FG%	REB	ASST
Behagen, Ron (3 years)	60	1170	213	90	516	8.6	.418	431	83
Boyd, Fred (4 years)	227	5997	998	505	2501	11.0	.424	1712	426
Coleman, E.C. (3 years)	47	1212	194	79	467	9.9	.478	90	147
	259	6148	927	361	2215	8.6	.403	424	791
	77	2369	290	82	662	8.6	.462	548	103
	202	5101	597	222	1416	7.0	.460	1220	268
Goodrich, Gail (11 years)	27	609	136	68	340	12.6	.446	61	74
Griffen, Paul	849	28,235	6393	3813	16,599	19.6	.454	2858	3986
	81	1645	140	145	425	5.2	.547	495	167
*Hansen, Glenn (1 year)	41	289	67	23	157	3.8	.432	59	25
**Howard, Mo	66	1145	173	85	431	6.5	.412	187	67
	32	345	64	24	152	4.8	.485	39	42
James, Aaron (2 years)	52	1059	238	89	565	10.9	.490	186	55
Kelley, Rich (1 year)	151	3077	632	300	1564	10.4	.461	615	125
	76	1505	184	156	524	6.9	.477	587	208
	75	1346	379	159	527	7.0	.485	528	53
Maravich, Pete (6 years)	73	3041	886	501	2273	31.1	.433	374	392
McElroy, Jim (1 year)	443	16,446	4065	2499	10,629	24.0	.415	1996	2510
	73	2029	301	169	771	10.6	.470	183	260
Moore, Otto (8 years)	51	1134	151	81	383	7.5	.510	110	107
	81	2084	193	91	477	5.9	.405	636	181
	601	14,809	2143	853	5159	8.6	.458	4939	879

	G	M	FGM	FTM	PTS	AVG	FG%	REB	ASST
***Robinson, Len (2 years)	77	2777	574	314	1462	19.0	.478	828	142
Stallworth, Bud (4 years)	158	3050	545	271	1361	8.6	.465	858	153
	40	526	126	17	269	6.7	.463	71	23
Walker, Andy	273	4963	895	344	2134	7.8	.408	790	190
	40	438	72	36	180	4.5	.462	75	32
Williams, Nate (5 years)	79	1776	414	146	974	12.3	.451	306	92
	409	10,545	2268	804	5340	13.1	.459	1752	736

*—Acquired from Kansas City
**—Combined Cleveland-New Orleans totals
***—Combined Washington-Atlanta totals; acquired from Atlanta

Most Promising Rookies: Essie Hollis, Tony Hanson. Hollis led St. Bonaventure to the National Invitation Tournament championship with a 21.8 scoring average in his senior year. The slender 6-6 forward is an extremely graceful player and has an excellent outside jumper. Hanson, a 6-4 guard, was the nation's 10th leading scorer with a 26-point average for the University of Connecticut.

PERFORMANCE QUOTIENTS

Offense: Maravich. In the past, that was the entire show. But the Jazz have added forward Robinson, who should average 20 points a game. The Jazz also are hoping guard Goodrich can come back from surgery on his Achilles tendon to regain his high-scoring form. If Essie Hollis earns a starting berth, the Jazz should have more offensive punch than in any time in their brief existence. Williams, James and McElroy each averaged in double figures for New Orleans last season. **Perf. Qt.: 4.**

Defense: In the past, whatever success the Jazz have had was the result of a solid team defense. But that aspect of New Orleans' game faltered last season as the Jazz gave up 107.4 points a game. Maravich and Goodrich are not going to win any awards for their defense. Moore continues to receive a great deal of playing time because of his defensive ability. **Perf. Qt.: 4.**

Rebounding: The Jazz were No. 2 in the NBA in rebounds last season, a remarkable statistic in view of the fact that New Orleans does not have a standout rebounder. Moore was the team's top rebounder with 636, but Kelley and Coleman each had more than 500. The acquisition of Robinson, who averaged more than 10 rebounds a game for the Atlanta Hawks, will strengthen the Jazz in this department. **Perf. Qt.: 2.**

Central Division

San Antonio Spurs

Prediction: Fifth

A serious attempt to analyze San Antonio's maiden season in the NBA somehow comes out sounding more like a sorry joke: Do you want to hear the good news first or the bad?

The good news is that the Spurs had the most explosive offense of any of the 22 teams, averaging 115 points per game; the bad news is that they also had the worst defense, giving back 114.4.

To all of which Coach Doug Moe provided his own punchline: "Defense? I thought the idea of the game was to outscore the other team."

San Antonio managed to do this often enough to turn in a respectable 44-38 record for third place in the Central Division, which is as well as could have been anticipated by the former ABA team. And the Spurs, despite being eliminated by Boston in the preliminary round of the playoffs, certainly were exciting to watch with their run 'n' gun attack. But obviously they will have to become more stingy at the other end of the court before they can be taken seriously.

For example, during one stretch of the season, San Antonio ran up point totals of 142, 137, 120, 127, 124 and 113, an average of 127.2 points, yet could do no better than a split of the six games. In two of those contests, the Spurs yielded 145 points at Denver and 150 at Portland.

"Everyone says we play poor defense because we give up so many points," Moe said. "But we press full-court all the time and try to get the other team into a running game. If we slowed down our offense, we wouldn't give up so many points, but we wouldn't score as much, either."

After signing a new contract for the 1977-78 campaign, Moe reasserted his faith in an explosive game. "The fast break was a big, big advantage to us last year, and the running game is something that we will continue to concentrate on in the future. About the defense, we will have to look at it and determine what is best for our players. I would say we will have to improve our overall defense."

Along with the best offense and the worst defense, the Spurs also had the distinction of being one of the unluckier teams in the NBA, a predicament that will continue to cost them in the new campaign. It goes back to the very first exhibition game when guard James Silas, the team captain and leading scorer the previous year, suffered a knee injury that required surgery. In an attempt to replace him, San Antonio traded away its first round draft choice to Los Angeles for Mack Calvin, another guard.

Calvin never got settled in San Antonio, wound up on the bench and eventually was placed on waivers.

As a result of this gamble, San Antonio had to fuss and fidget on the sidelines until the 37th pick in the collegiate draft, when it took another gamble by selecting a little-known 7-foot center, Jeff Wilkins, who averaged 21.8 points per game as a senior at Illinois State.

PREDICTION: FIFTH 61

This was the second consecutive year the Texans were unable to strengthen themselves with a top collegian. In 1976, when the four ABA survivors joined the NBA, one of the conditions was that they wouldn't participate in the draft.

San Antonio recognized its biggest need up front, and another big man who will be contending for a job is 6-9, 230-pound Rick Bullock, a native of the Alamo city who was cut by the Knicks the day before the 1976 season started. Bullock, described by the Spurs' brass as "a big, strong player who can shoot well and who can go to the boards with authority," was the all-time leading scorer at Texas Tech with 2,117 points, a 19.6 career average.

With Silas limited to 22 games, San Antonio had to revamp its offense and the thrust of the scoring burden fell to George Gervin, a 6-7 swingman, and 6-9 forward Larry Kenon, who averaged 45 points a game between them. Kenon also was the team leader in rebounds with 879.

Gervin was a forward until Moe shifted him to the backcourt in what was supposed to be a stopgap move until Silas returned. But after watching him perform for a while, Moe gushed, "I think George Gervin is the most valuable guard in the league. I know all about Pete Maravich and the others, but anytime you've got a guard making 54 per cent of his shots, especially when all the defenses are designed to stop him, you have something special."

Apparently, there were enough unbiased observers who agreed since Gervin, with his 23.1 average, was selected to the second NBA All-Star team as a guard.

"I love it there," said Gervin, who ran up a streak of 78 consecutive double figure scoring games before it was snapped by Atlanta. "It's a big advantage to have me in the backcourt. I can get a lot of offensive rebounds and also get my man in foul trouble."

Gervin generally started alongside 6-4 Mike Gale, an excellent ball-handler who led the team with 473 assists, eighth best in the league.

Kenon, a skinny, 6-9, 195-pounder, wasn't exactly encouraged to shoot much when he played alongside Julius Erving on the New York Nets. With San Antonio, he says, "I'm getting a chance to exploit my talents," and he gives a lot of credit to Gervin.

"We communicate better than J [Erving] and I did," said Kenon, who averaged 21.9 points. "G [Gervin] respects my talent more and he would come to me quicker in a tough situation than J would anytime. I always got along with J, but we weren't as close as I am with G."

In addition to his scoring and rebounding exploits, Kenon set an NBA record last December when he was credited with 11 steals against Kansas City. Kenon finished the season with 167, second on the team to Gale's 191.

The center chores last season were shared by a pair of 6-11 giants, Billy Paultz and Coby Dietrick. Paultz, who lost 20 pounds during the summer of 1976, reporting to camp at a svelte 240, averaged 15.6 points and was second in rebounding with 687. He also ranked ninth in the NBA with 173 blocked shots. Dietrick, also used at forward, averaged 8.4 points and had 372 rebounds.

Also averaging in double figures last season were forwards Allan Bristow (11.4) and Mark Olberding (10.4), but Bristow played out his option and wasn't expected to return this season.

"Looking back, it was fun," Moe summarized.

PREDICTION: FIFTH

Statistics for 1976-77 season

Player's name — Years in NBA prior to 1976-77

Career statistics, not including those of the 1976-77 season

Player	G	M	FGM	FTM	PTS	AVG	FG%	REB	ASST
Bristow, Allan †(2 years)	82	2017	365	206	936	11.4	.489	348	240
Dampier, Louie †(9 years)	127	1744	271	163	705	5.6	.409	421	191
Dietrick, Coby †(6 years)	80	1634	233	64	530	6.6	.460	76	234
Gale, Mike †(5 years)	728	27,770	5290	2352	13,726	18.9	.457	2282	4084
Gervin, George †(4 years)	82	1772	285	119	689	8.4	.460	372	148
Karl, George	362	7046	940	342	2225	6.1	.457	1903	750
Kenon, Larry †(3 years)	82	2598	353	137	843	10.3	.468	273	473
Olberding, Mark †(1 year)	389	9456	1191	436	2831	7.3	.460	1323	1181
Paultz, Billy †(6 years)	82	2705	726	443	1895	23.1	.544	454	238
Silas, James †(4 years)	269	9061	2323	1196	5887	21.9	.491	1977	584
Ward, Henry †(1 year)	29	251	25	29	79	2.7	.342	17	46
	231	4168	647	312	1618	7.0	.483	347	744
	78	2936	706	293	1705	21.9	.492	879	229
	249	8993	1912	594	4419	17.7	.485	2759	385
	82	1949	301	251	853	10.4	.503	449	119
	81	2055	302	191	795	9.8	.498	530	142
	82	2694	521	238	1280	15.6	.473	687	223
	487	16,762	3149	1369	7667	15.7	.503	5406	1163
	22	356	61	87	209	9.5	.430	32	50
	328	11,730	2123	1732	5978	18.2	.504	1324	1413
	27	171	34	15	83	3.1	.378	33	6
	61	688	154	16	330	5.4	.477	140	35

†—ABA totals

Most Promising Rookies: Rick Bullock, Jeff Wilkins. Bullock, a high school star in San Antonio and the all-time leading scorer at Texas Tech, is getting another big chance in his hometown. A year ago, the 6-9, 230-pound forward was drafted in the fourth round by the Knicks, who waived him the day before the season started. At Texas Tech, where he scored 2117 points for a 19.6 career average, Bullock was called "the franchise" by his coach, Gerald Myers. "Rick was the best player in Tech basketball history," Myers said. "He was very unselfish and very physical, and he probably can be a better pro player than he was a college player." Wilkins, the 37th player chosen in the draft, is a 7-foot center who averaged 21.8 points last season at Illinois State.

PERFORMANCE QUOTIENTS

Offense: If the Spurs felt they had to prove they belonged in the NBA, they certainly went about it in flamboyant style. Emphasizing a run 'n' gun attack, San Antonio had the most explosive offense in the league, running up an average of 115 points per game, almost 2½ points better than runnerup Denver, another former ABA team. The Spurs also were second in field goal percentage with a .485 mark. Coach Doug Moe stresses a running game, and says he will continue to do so. Strangely, the Spurs wreaked most of their havoc with little service from the injured Silas, who was their leading scorer the previous year. Silas, with a career average of 18.2 in the ABA, was limited to 22 games and contributed only 356 points, an average of 9.5. Gervin, equally effective as a forward or guard, and Kenon assumed most of the scoring load with averages of 23.1 and 21.9, respectively, giving San Antonio ninth and 11th places in the NBA scoring race. Paultz, Bristow, Olberding and Gale also hit in double figures. More offensive help may be forthcoming from free agent Rick Bullock. **Perf. Qt.: 1.**

Defense: Far more generous than is good for any pro team, San Antonio gave back just as quickly at one end of the court what it took at the other. The Spurs had the most porous defense in the league, yielding a woeful 114.4 points a game, causing Moe to understate, "I would say we will have to improve our overall defense." Paultz was among the league leaders in blocked shots with 173 as was Gale in steals with 191. Kenon, a fine all-around performer, had 167 steals while Gervin had 105 steals and 104 blocked shots. **Perf. Qt.: 5.**

Rebounding: Only two teams gathered in fewer than the 3660 rebounds totaled by the Spurs, although their big men did have fewer opportunities off the offensive board because of all the scoring. Still, help is needed up front, and it is unlikely that the 6-9, 230-pound Bullock will provide the whole solution. Kenon, despite his slender build, was the leading Spur rebounder with 879, followed by Paultz with 687 and Gervin with 454. **Perf. Qt.: 4.**

Central Division

Atlanta Hawks

Prediction: Sixth

On the day after he was suspended for one year by Baseball Commissioner Bowie Kuhn, Ted Turner went out and bought controlling interest in the Atlanta Hawks. Turner's first official act was to bring in Mike Storen as a stockholder and managing partner, following which Storen observed, "It's really fun to sit down with your new partner and learn he's been suspended for the good of sports."

If you're an Atlanta sports fan—and the species is becoming near extinct—you can feel assured that Turner, a renegade yachtsman turned sports entrepreneur, will be good for the Hawks. Despite his suspension by Kuhn for tampering, Turner injected an aura of excitement into the baseball Braves, who also had been a withering franchise, and he promises to do the same in basketball.

He showed his good intentions by turning over operation of the club to Storen, a basketball-wise veteran of the War Between the Leagues. Storen, a still-young 42, operated three teams in the old American Basketball Association and in 1973-74 served as the league's commissioner.

A man who thrived on the cutthroat rivalry with the

NBA, Storen noted with a touch of sadness soon after joining the Hawks how much more difficult it is now to build a contender. "You don't have the advantage now of being able to go and steal players from the other league," he said. "Your draft takes on added importance, and there is luck involved."

Hawk fans know only too well the vagaries of the draft. Two years in a row Atlanta owned the rights to the No. 1 collegiate pick, but didn't get to sign either player. Two years ago, in fact, the Hawks had the first and third choices overall, selecting David Thompson and Marvin Webster, and lost both to Denver. A year ago, perhaps a little gunshy, they dealt the No. 1 pick in the nation to Houston for reserve center Joe Meriweather.

This past spring, Atlanta didn't have to face such a trauma. For the first time in three years the Hawks didn't own the top choice, but at least they did sign their first-round pick, the 14th player selected. (They chose in this spot because of a trade with Washington.) And they were delighted to find that 7-1, 235-pound Wayne Rollins, aptly called "Tree," still was available.

"I wouldn't call Rollins a franchise," said Coach Hubie Brown. "There are only two of those in basketball, and they're both on the West Coast [an obvious reference to Kareem Abdul-Jabbar and Bill Walton]. But I'm very happy because he was our top choice at the center position. And the fact we signed him is a great plus."

At Clemson last season, Rollins averaged four blocked shots a game as well as 12.8 rebounds, but he never was a proficient scorer. His 14.1 scoring average as a senior was the best of his four-year career.

Without doubt, on a team full of holes, the Hawks' most pressing need was for a dominating center. Playing the pivot last season were Meriweather, a slender 6-10 who didn't provide enough board strength, Steve Hawes, who was limited to 44 games because of a broken shin bone, and rookie Tom Barker, a fourth-round draft choice from Hawaii. Of them only Meriweather, at 11.1, was able to average in double figures.

If Rollins can handle the center job, Meriweather, Hawes and Barker will compete for the forward positions, with the loser providing strong backup support at both center and forward.

Last season the Hawks finished in last place in the Central Division with a 31-51 record, the fourth worst in the NBA and only two games better than their mark in the previous campaign, their poorest in 22 years.

The snake-bit character of the Hawks is illustrated by another unfortunate turn of events. Two weeks after Turner bought the faltering franchise, Atlanta made a deal with Washington, sending playmaking guard Tom Henderson to the Bullets for the man called "Truck" Robinson.

Robinson, a 6-7 bull of a forward, averaged 22.4 points in his 36 games with Atlanta (19.0 overall for the season), second on the club only to John Drew, and his total of 828 rebounds was by far the best on the team. Robinson made such a difference upon joining the Hawks that they won 14 of their first 25 games with him in the lineup before a string of injuries wiped out the guard corps and left Atlanta without outside shooting capability.

Although he was leaving a perennial playoff contender, Robinson expressed happiness at the deal that sent him to Atlanta. He claimed that in almost three years with the Bullets, they never designed any plays to get him the ball, while in Atlanta "we play my type of ball here and I'm much more relaxed. I know I'm going to play 40 minutes every night and I'm really getting in the groove." But then, not long after the season ended, he exercised his option and signed with New Orleans, dealing a severe blow to the Hawks' rebuilding plans.

A significant positive side effect of the Robinson-Henderson deal was the chance for Armond Hill, a first-round draft choice last year, to show his skills as the club's playmaker. Hill averaged only six points a game, but he led the team with 403 assists, evidence enough that he can handle the job if he gets the kind of people up front who can put the ball in the basket. Last year the Hawks averaged 102.4 points per game, the fourth poorest figure in the league.

The backcourt would be strengthened immeasurably if high-scoring veteran Geoff Petrie can return from knee surgery. Petrie and Hawes were obtained from Portland last year in return for the rights to Maurice Lucas in the ABA dispersal draft. With Lucas a vital cog, the Trail Blazers went on to win the NBA championship while Petrie was forced to sit out the entire campaign.

The scoring leader is Drew, an indomitable free spirit. The 6-7 forward has shown steady improvement in his three years in the NBA, and his 24.2 average last season placed him seventh in the league scoring race. He also had 675 rebounds, second on the team to Robinson, and 102 steals.

"We've got a great young team for the future and the kids know we're going to be good," Brown said late last season. "We're the youngest team in the NBA and I'm very optimistic about the future." That, though, was before the defection of Robinson.

PREDICTION: SIXTH

Statistics for 1976-77 season

Career statistics, not including those of the 1976-77 season

Player's name / Years in NBA prior to 1976-77	G	M	FGM	FTM	PTS	AVG	FG%	REB	ASST
Barker, Tom	59	1354	182	112	476	8.1	.417	401	60
Brown, John (3 years)	77	1405	160	121	441	5.7	.457	236	103
Charles, Ken (3 years)	225	5459	807	510	2124	9.4	.448	1278	373
Denton, Randy (3 years)	82	2487	354	205	913	11.1	.414	168	295
†(5 years)	219	4630	656	334	1646	7.5	.462	448	429
Drew, John (2 years)	45	700	103	33	239	5.3	.402	218	33
Hawes, Steve (2 years)	368	9484	1932	643	4510	12.3	.478	3329	495
Hill, Armond	74	2688	689	412	1790	24.2	.487	675	133
	155	4640	1113	876	3102	20.0	.464	1496	288
	44	945	147	67	361	8.2	.482	261	63
	127	2308	339	132	810	6.4	.497	772	203
	81	1825	175	139	489	6.0	.399	143	403
Hudson, Lou (10 years)	58	1745	413	142	968	16.7	.456	129	155
Meriweather, Joe (1 year)	672	24,080	6157	2767	15,081	22.4	.489	3469	1943
Sojourner, Mike (2 years)	74	2068	319	182	820	11.1	.526	596	82
*Terry, Claude	81	2042	338	154	830	10.2	.494	516	82
†(4 years)	51	551	95	41	231	4.5	.468	146	21
	140	3731	626	175	1427	10.2	.482	1091	151
	45	545	96	36	228	5.1	.503	46	58
	277	3592	658	284	1647	5.9	.483	438	392

ATLANTA HAWKS

	G	M	FGM	FTM	PTS	AVG	FG%	REB	ASST
Willoughby, Bill (1 year)	39	549	75	43	193	4.9	.444	170	13
—Combined Buffalo-Atlanta totals	62	870	113	66	292	4.7	.398	288	31
†—ABA totals									

Most Promising Rookies: Wayne Rollins, Sam Smith, Ed Johnson. There is some question in other camps whether Rollins will be good enough as a pro to make a difference on a weak club. But he is 7-1, weighs 235 pounds, and the Hawks were delighted he still was available when their turn came in the draft. Smith and Johnson both are guards with strong shooting credentials. Smith, who is 6-4, played at the University of Nevada-Las Vegas while the 6-1 Johnson averaged 15.6 points at Auburn last season with 135 assists. Both Smith and Johnson were drafted on the third round, although Brown feels they were second round quality.

PERFORMANCE QUOTIENTS

Offense: For all the changes in the roster, there is still little zip in the Atlanta attack, and until the Hawks add some punch, they are going to continue having trouble zapping other teams. Once again the Hawks had the fourth poorest offense in the league, an average of 102.4 points per game. Hurting Atlanta was the loss for the entire 1976-77 campaign of Geoff Petrie, one of the better shooting guards in the NBA, and Hudson, who was limited to 58 games. Hurting them in 1977-78 will be the absence of Len "Truck" Robinson, who defected to New Orleans. Apparently, it will be up to Petrie and Hudson to lift the offense this season since Atlanta didn't claim a devastating scorer in the draft. Of course, 7-1 Tree Rollins can help the attack by picking off those offensive rebounds. With Hudson hurting, Drew has developed into the team scoring leader, averaging 24.2 points last season. **Perf. Qt.: 5.**

Defense: The defense also slipped from the previous year as Atlanta yielded a per game average of 106.4 points, but this should improve with the addition of Rollins. The 6-10 Meriweather, who is slender, slipped from 120 blocked shots in 1975-76 to 82, which was still the club high, indicating a lack of intimidation on defense. Hill and Charles are adequate defensive guards, but it is up to Rollins to provide any drastic improvement. **Perf. Qt.: 4.**

Rebounding: This was another weak category for the Hawks last season, and here, too, Robinson will be missed. The team's total of 2512 defensive rebounds was the fourth lowest in the league. Again, it will be left to the raw rookie, Rollins, to pick up the board game. Also helping will be Drew, who had 675 and Meriweather 596. Hawes had 261 rebounds in only 44 games, and his return to full strength would be welcome. **Perf. Qt.: 4.**

Midwest Division

Denver Nuggets

Prediction: First

Denver Nuggets Coach Larry Brown motivates his players better than any other coach in the National Basketball Association. That may be his problem.

For three straight years now, the Nuggets have battled through the regular season like champions and then have done a Duane Bobick in the playoffs. In fairness, it should be pointed out that the Nuggets' last two playoff failures have been against the eventual champions—the New York Nets and the Portland Trail Blazers.

Still, the Nuggets have built a firm foundation for becoming known as basketball's answer to the Minnesota Vikings.

The Nuggets' inaugural season in the NBA was a successful one as Denver won the Midwest Division title with a 50-32 record.

"Night in and night out, our team plays up to our potential as well as anyone else," Brown said.

That could be the answer to the Nuggets' sudden demise in the playoffs. Perhaps they are putting together such an outstanding regular season record because they are trying. Certainly, there are one or two players around the league who consider their job going through the motions and collecting their weekly paycheck until the playoffs begin.

The Nuggets are not going to improve dramatically in the playoffs as several other teams with malingerers might.

Still, in their first season, the Nuggets proved themselves to be one of the most talented teams in the NBA. They were practically unbeatable in the rarified Denver air, compiling a 36-5 home record, second only to the Los Angeles Lakers' NBA record of 37-4.

"I didn't know what to expect," Brown said of his team's debut in the NBA. As to the Nuggets' excellent start in the NBA, he said, "I am surprised because we didn't get to draft any college players. Plus, we didn't get any players in the dispersal draft either."

But the Nuggets' bubble burst against the Trail Blazers and, with Denver on the ropes, forward Bobby Jones said, "The spirit isn't here anymore."

"After this thing is over, I'm backing the truck up," said Brown, indicating there would be some drastic changes in personnel. He kept his word, too. In a three-way deal with the Seattle SuperSonics and the Kansas City Kings, Denver traded forwards Willie Wise and Paul Silas and center Marvin Webster to Seattle. In exchange, the Nuggets received guard Bobby Wilkerson and center Tom Burleson. Burleson then was dispatched to Kansas City for guard Brian Taylor.

The Nuggets' surplus of forwards and need for a guard, which motivated the trade, was created by David Thompson's return to the forward position after an experiment in the backcourt.

When Thompson graduated from North Carolina State, his detractors said he was too small at 6-3 to play forward in the pros and not quick enough or a good enough outside shooter to make it as a guard. In his first season in the NBA, Thompson proved himself a superstar at either position, although he expressed a preference for forward.

"At the forward position I feel more comfortable," said the league's most spectacular leaper. "I don't have to bring the ball up or apply defensive pressure from baseline to baseline."

Thompson connected on 50.7 per cent of his field goal attempts to average 25.9 points a game and finish as the league's fourth leading scorer. In addition, he led the Nuggets with 337 assists and had 53 blocked shots.

Thompson was selected to the NBA's All-Star team, the only newcomer from the ABA to earn first-team honors.

Dan Issel and Bobby Jones also proved their ABA reputations were not undeserved. Issel, the 6-10 center, had a scoring average of 22.3 to give the Nuggets the greatest one-two scoring punch in the league. Together, Thompson and Issel averaged 48.2 points a game, with Indiana's Billy Knight and John Williamson next at 47.4.

Jones, hailed by many as the top defensive forward in the game, was the league's third leading field goal percentage shooter. He sank 57 per cent of his shots for a scoring average of 15.1. He ranked sixth in the league in steals with an average of 2.27, the best mark for a forward.

At the conclusion of the season, Jones received one national award as the league's top all-around player. A computer picked him ahead of the official Most Valuable Player, Kareem Abdul-Jabbar of Los Angeles.

"Typically modest, Jones said of the runnerup: "Kareem's more of a floor leader. Even when he's not scoring, he's on the court, doing other things and building confidence in the team."

The Nuggets' backcourt of Mack Calvin, Ted McClain, Fatty Taylor and Jim Price did a passable job, but Denver strengthened itself considerably with the addition of Brian Taylor.

Taylor, outstanding offensively and defensively, averaged 17 points a game for the Kings and was second in the league in steals with 2.76 a game. He also had 320 assists. The 6-6 Wilkerson, who started for Indiana's 1976 NCAA championship team, gives the Nuggets a big defensive guard who also can be moved up to forward occasionally.

As for replacing the rebounding strength of Silas and Webster, the Nuggets are hoping for a lot of help from No. 1 draft pick Tom LaGarde and free agent Jacky Dorsey.

LaGarde, from Brown's alma mater, North Carolina, was a member of the gold medal winning U.S. Olympic team and the 6-10 forward did surprisingly well in the rough international ball. Although not nearly as talented as Jones, LaGarde was drilled in the team concept by North Carolina Coach Dean Smith and should fit in well at Denver.

Dorsey was a second-round draft choice of the New Orleans Jazz in 1976 after going hardship before his junior year at the University of Georgia. Waived by the Jazz, the 6-7, 230-pound Dorsey played with Hartford in the Eastern Basketball League and made the All-League team by averaging 21.9 points and 11.1 rebounds a game.

"Jacky is a physically gifted athlete, but he lacked maturity last season when he signed with the Jazz," Brown said.

PREDICTION: FIRST 75

Player's name — Statistics for 1976-77 season

Years in NBA prior to 1976-77	G	M	FGM	FTM	PTS	AVG	FG%	REB	ASST
Beck, Byron	53	480	107	36	250	4.7	.435	96	33
†(9 years)	694	18,717	3574	1192	8353	12.0	.508	5165	939
*Calvin, Mack	76	1438	220	287	727	9.6	.404	96	240
†(7 years)	533	18,267	3502	3554	10,620	19.9	.458	1647	1613
Issel, Dan	79	2507	660	1282	1765	22.3	.515	696	177
†(6 years)	500	19,444	4507	2799	12,823	25.6	.490	5426	1103
Jones, Bobby	82	2419	501	236	1238	15.1	.570	678	264
†(6 years)	..167	5551	1039	402	2480	14.9	.593	1483	634
McClain, Ted	72	2002	245	99	589	8.2	.445	229	324
†(5 years)	377	9196	1419	746	3611	9.6	.460	1217	1368
**Price, Jim	81	1828	253	83	589	7.3	.446	231	261
(4 years)	271	7851	1411	557	3379	12.5	.437	952	1147
Taylor, Brian	72	2488	501	225	1227	17.0	.504	238	320
†(4 years)	271	1887	1284	582	3804	14.0	.511	811	1002
Taylor, Fatty	79	1548	132	37	301	3.8	.420	211	288
†(7 years)	561	16,447	1831	1106	4797	8.6	.448	2313	2275
Thompson, David	82	3001	824	477	2125	25.9	.507	334	337
†(1 year)	83	3101	807	541	2158	26.0	.519	525	308
Towe, Monty	51	409	56	18	130	2.5	.406	34	87
†(1 year)	64	576	72	36	189	3.0	.519	55	136
Wilkerson, Bobby	78	1552	221	84	528	6.7	.386	258	171

*—Combined Los Angeles-San Antonio-Denver totals †—ABA totals
**—Combined Buffalo-Denver totals

Most Promising Rookies: Tom LaGarde, Anthony Roberts, Robert Smith. LaGarde, 6-10, played center and forward at North Carolina. North Carolina products Mitch Kupchak and Bobby Jones were second and third in the NBA last season in field goal percentage, so LaGarde can be expected to choose his shots wisely. He also proved to be surprisingly tough under the boards in the Olympics. Roberts, the nation's second leading scorer with a 34-point average for Oral Roberts, had a record 65 points in a National Invitation Tournament game. Smith was the one player in the Nevada-Las Vegas lineup able to pass the ball without cringing. His extreme quickness made him a defensive asset and he led the nation in free throw percentage.

PERFORMANCE QUOTIENTS

Offense: The Nuggets were the second leading offensive team in the NBA last season and should be even better this season with the addition of guard Brian Taylor. The Nuggets gave up Marvin Webster and Paul Silas to get Taylor, but their chief contributions to Denver were not on offense anyway. Thompson and Issel provided the best one-two scoring punch in the NBA and Jones was the third best in field goal percentage. Thompson, who can go to the hoop or shoot from outside, averaged 25.9 points. Issel is one of the best outside shooting big men in the league and had a 22.3 average. Jones averaged 15.1 and the Nuggets' front line starters each shot better than 50 per cent. Calvin had been the Nuggets' top scoring guard with an 11.1 average, but Taylor can get them 20 points a night from the backcourt. Taylor averaged 17 points a game for Kansas City by sinking 50 per cent of his shots. And he also is excellent at running an offense. **Perf. Qt.: 1.**

Defense: Jones is earning a reputation as the best defensive forward in basketball. He averaged 2.27 steals a game to lead all NBA forwards. Issel and Thompson do not embarrass themselves defensively, but are not among the league's best either. This is another area in which Brian Taylor will be a help. McClain, Price and Fatty Taylor also are good defensive guards. **Perf. Qt.: 3.**

Rebounding: The Nuggets were one of the top rebounding teams in the NBA, but this is where they will feel the loss of Silas and Webster, who combined for 1090 rebounds. Jones and Issel will have to take up some of the slack, and if Tom LaGarde doesn't come through with some help, the Nuggets could be in trouble. **Perf. Qt.: 3.**

Midwest Division

Chicago Bulls

Prediction: Second

Ed Badger appeared a sure-shot to join such National Basketball Association coaching legends as Carl Bennett, Scotty Robertson and Mike Farmer. These men were legends in their own time because their own time in the NBA was so remarkably brief, marked with an outstanding lack of success.

Bennett was 0-6 in the Fort Wayne Pistons' first season; Robertson got the New Orleans Jazz off to a 1-14 start, and Farmer was 1-8 in his fling with the Baltimore Bullets. But somehow Badger managed to avoid joining this group, despite a horrendous start, and the Chicago Bulls made a sterling comeback to reach the NBA playoffs.

"I read I was gone so many times early in the season that if I had a lease I couldn't have gotten it renewed," Badger said.

Badger had been Dick Motta's assistant with the Bulls and got the top job when Motta went to the Washington Bullets. Badger was taking over a team which had finished with a 24-58 record, the result of the worst offense in the NBA. But a drastic improvement was expected after the Bulls added Scott May, the 1976 College Player of the Year, then picked up

7-2 Artis Gilmore in the American Basketball Association dispersal draft. Certainly the Bulls were expected to improve their 95.9 scoring average and .414 field goal percentage, the worst in the NBA.

Then, May and Jack Marin came down with mononucleosis at the beginning of the season and Gilmore failed to set the NBA aglow with his talent in the first two months.

Chicago lost 14 of its first 16 games and was zero for the month of November. But May got healthy, free agent guard Wilbur Holland was a valuable addition and Gilmore began paying dividends on the $1-million the Bulls paid for the privilege of picking up his contract. By the end of the regular season, the Bulls were playing as well as anyone in the league and won 20 of their final 24 games to qualify for the playoffs with a 44-38 record.

"I felt all along that we could make a run for the playoffs if we ever got our team together," said Badger, whose biggest worry must have been whether he would be around for the playoffs. "You have to remember we went through a lot in the first month of the season."

Guard Norm Van Lier remembered, "We had guys with mono and Jerry Sloan couldn't come back from knee surgery. And Gilmore was having trouble adjusting, so we were hurting."

Center Tom Boerwinkle explained the problems the Bulls were trying to overcome during the early part of the season.

"It was a while before all our people were here and healthy," Boerwinkle said. "Then we had to adjust. For 10 years this team was oriented toward a non-shooting, non-running center—me. Then we got Artis and put him with 11 guys he'd never even seen before. Now he's playing better than any center in the league."

The Bulls' tremendous resurgence finally was halted in the playoffs by the Portland Trail Blazers, the eventual champions, but Chicago demonstrated the rebuilding job was finished for the most part and the Bulls are ready to begin raking in the dividends.

Gilmore connected on 52 per cent of his shots to lead the Bulls in scoring with an 18.6 average and was the league's fourth leading rebounder with an average of 13. He also was fourth in blocked shots and his imposing presence on the inside played a key role in Chicago's ranking as the NBA's top defensive team for the third straight year.

Slender forward Mickey Johnson continued as one of the most unheralded stars in the game with an average of 17.3 points and 10.2 rebounds a game and May brought his scoring average up to 14.6 by the end of the season to give the Bulls a solid front line.

Undoubtedly, the addition of Holland was a major factor in the Bulls' midseason form reversal. After being cut by the Atlanta Hawks, the 6-foot guard was picked up by the Bulls and proved the perfect backcourt complement to defensive wizard Van Lier. Holland sank 45 per cent of his field goal attempts, mostly long-range missiles, to average 14.9 points a game, and Van Lier had a 10.2 average.

The Bulls also acquired Kamikaze Kid John Mengelt from the Detroit Pistons and the solidly built guard averaged 8.3 points a game. The massive Boerwinkle may have had his career prolonged several years by the addition of Gilmore. Although his playing time was cut considerably, Boerwinkle was more than adequate during his brief relief appearances for Gilmore and could continue in that role for a long time.

Duke guard Tate Armstrong, one of the best outside shooters in the nation, was Chicago's No. 1 draft pick and the Bulls selected another outstanding guard in Southern Illinois' Mike Glenn. The next two players selected by the Bulls were Maryland forward Steve Sheppard and Arizona State forward Mark Landsberger. Armstrong and Sheppard won gold medals with the U.S. Olympic basketball team in Montreal, while Landsberger was the last player cut.

Certainly the Bulls will receive some help from that group, but a great deal of improvement does not seem necessary for Chicago to make a serious run for the NBA title. It's highly unlikely the Bulls will feel the need to spot their rivals such a giant head start this season.

Certainly, one of the improvements Badger brought the Bulls was in attitude. Even Van Lier, a perpetual malcontent under Motta, was at peace with the world.

"I love these people," Van Lier said of a group of Bulls fans asking for his autograph. "It was no secret that I didn't get along with Dick Motta. When I got suspended, Motta didn't back me up, the fans did. I got fined $1000 and the fans paid it. I belong to Chicago. That's why I do anything to win.

"And while we're winning, I think about the Bulls who aren't playing now—Jerry Sloan, Chet Walker, Matt Guokas. As long as I'm playing, a part of them will be out there too because they're all a part of me."

When Van Lier can sound so positively enchanted, the Chicago Bulls can be sure they're in great shape.

Now if Ed Badger makes his name noteworthy in the NBA annals, it will be for winning a championship.

PREDICTION: SECOND

Statistics for 1976-77 season

Player's name Years in NBA prior to 1976-77	G	M	FGM	FTM	PTS	AVG	FG%	REB	ASST
Boerwinkle, Tom (8 years)	82	1070	134	34	302	3.7	.491	312	189
Gilmore, Artis	531	13,090	1706	826	4238	8.0	.451	5374	1774
†(5 years)	82	2877	570	387	1527	18.6	.522	1070	199
*Hicks, Phil	420	17,449	3671	2018	9362	22.3	.558	7169	1273
	37	262	41	11	93	2.5	.461	66	24
Holland, Wilbur	79	2453	509	158	1176	14.9	.454	253	253
(1 year)	33	351	85	22	192	5.8	.399	41	26
Johnson, Mickey (2 years)	81	2847	583	324	1400	17.3	.446	828	195
Kropp, Tom	119	2681	531	320	1382	11.6	.461	852	152
(1 year)	53	480	73	28	174	3.3	.480	47	39
Laskowski, John	25	72	7	5	19	0.8	.233	15	8
(1 year)	47	562	75	27	177	3.8	.354	63	44
May, Scott	71	1570	284	87	655	9.2	.412	219	55
	72	2369	431	188	1050	14.6	.451	437	145
Mengelt, John	61	1178	209	89	507	8.3	.456	110	114
(5 years)	381	7740	1456	920	3832	10.1	.477	841	756
Pondexter, Cliff	78	996	107	42	256	3.3	.416	236	41
(1 year)	75	1326	156	122	434	5.8	.411	381	90
Starr, Keith	17	65	6	2	14	0.8	.250	10	6

CHICAGO BULLS

	G	M	FGM	FTM	PTS	AVG	FG%	REB	ASST
Van Lier, Norm (7 years)	82	3097	300	238	838	10.2	.412	370	636
*—Combined Houston-Chicago totals	548	19,995	2783	1678	7253	13.2	.414	2902	3892

†—ABA totals

Most Promising Rookies: Tate Armstrong, Mike Glenn, Steve Sheppard. In Armstrong and Glenn the Bulls picked up two of the finest shooting guards in the country. Armstrong was injured early in his senior year at Duke, but had made the U.S. Olympic team chiefly on his great shooting ability. Glenn, who attended Southern Illinois, invariably has been compared to fellow alum Walt Frazier and has not fared poorly in the comparisons. A slick ball-handler, Glenn also has an unerring touch. Sheppard, a 6-5 forward, would appear to be a longshot to make the Bulls, but he was in a similar situation entering the U.S. Olympic tryouts and was the most impressive player in camp.

PERFORMANCE QUOTIENTS

Offense: The Bulls again finished as the second lowest scoring team in the league, but they picked up considerably when May regained his health and Gilmore became acclimated to the NBA. Gilmore led the Bulls in scoring with an 18.6 average and was awesome at times. But the 7-foot-2 center has been inconsistent throughout his career and he's not going to change now. Slender forward Johnson, who averaged 17.3 points, has become much more effective with the addition of Gilmore. May, after his early-season illness, averaged 14.6 points and should improve that figure this season. The Bulls gained some badly needed scoring in the backcourt when they picked up free agent Holland. Holland had a 14.9 average and Van Lier averaged 10.2. Perf. Qt.: 3.

Defense: As with the offense, the Bulls' defense must center around Gilmore. The giant defender blocked 203 shots to finish fourth in the league. The Bulls also added another fine defensive player in May. Thus, is it any surprise the Bulls finished as the NBA's best defensive team for the third straight year? Van Lier claims to be the best defensive guard in basketball and many will agree with him. Perf. Qt.: 1.

Rebounding: Only three teams collected more rebounds than the Bulls, and Chicago held its opponents to fewer rebounds than anyone else. Gilmore was the league's fourth leading rebounder and Johnson is deceptively strong. This is one area in which May should improve greatly this season. Perf. Qt.: 2.

Midwest Division

Detroit Pistons

Prediction: Third

Whatever Herb Brown gets paid to coach the Detroit Pistons, it's not enough to compensate for having to tolerate the antics of pro basketball's answer to Romper Room.

Two National Basketball Association coaches said last season Detroit had more talent than any team in the league, including the Philadelphia 76ers, but the Pistons finished with only a 44-38 record and were eliminated from the playoffs by the Golden State Warriors.

The Pistons have four good guards who keep the team in a continual state of rebellion because only two of them can play at one time. The Pistons have one of the truly outstanding big centers in the league in Bob Lanier, who complains about the incessant gripes, grunts and groans of his teammates and threatens to leave the team because of them. Finally, the Pistons have Marvin Barnes, the most sensitive convict in the NBA.

Brown is supposed to coach this crew and, consequently, is the focal point of their rage.

"They're not angry at me," insists Brown, the brother

of Denver Coach Larry Brown. "Any coach would have the problem.

"You got Kevin Porter, who came here to replace the most popular guy ever to play in Detroit [Dave Bing]. Porter gets hurt and has to prove himself all over again. You got [Eric] Money, 22 years old, third year in the league. He knows he's a starter. Chris Ford is playing the best ball of his life and [Ralph] Simpson is an All-Star.

"Everyone's all over me because I'm the easiest one to get. Listen, I'm a jerk before I even walk out on the court, so what do I have to lose? I'm paid to win and I think it's better to have everyone talking than to have it all boiling up inside. At least we're loose."

The entire team was so loose Lanier kept threatening to take his 25.3 scoring average and 745 rebounds and go home, a la Dave Cowens.

"This stuff's ridiculous," Lanier said. "It never should have been allowed to get started in the first place. If it gets to where I can't deal with it, I'm going to have to leave the game a while."

Lanier never did follow through on his threats, but missed 18 games because of injuries. During his absence, rookie Leon Douglas filled in admirably. Playing in all 82 regular season games, Douglas averaged 7.5 points a game, sinking 48 per cent of his shots, and grabbed 526 rebounds.

If Barnes turned out to be the booby prize from the ABA, the Pistons received a pleasant surprise from forward M.L. Carr. The 6-6 Carr had been waived by the Kansas City Kings and the Boston Celtics before catching on with the Spirits of St. Louis for the 1975-76 season and averaging 12.2 points a game. Carr played out his option with the Spirits and the Pistons signed him as a free agent even before the merger was accomplished. Surprisingly, Carr stepped right into the starting lineup and was the Pistons' second leading scorer with a 13.3 average and had 631 rebounds.

The much-traveled Howard Porter held onto a starting position for the first time in his career and averaged 13.2 points a game opposite Carr on the front line.

Carr and Howard Porter benefited from the exploits of the remarkable Mr. Barnes. The 6-9 Barnes, who averaged 24 points a game with St. Louis and is potentially one of the best forwards in pro basketball, jumped ship and demanded the Pistons renegotiate his contract. Barnes is the highly principled young man who came out of Providence and said he would not play basketball for a penny less than $1-million, that he would rather work in a factory. After Barnes got his million dollars in a multi-year contract and spent a great deal of his salary on frivolities, he walked out on the Spirits and demanded they renegotiate his contract. He lost that battle, so he decided to give it another shot with the Pistons. While staging his one-man strike, Barnes was arrested in the Detroit airport for attempting to carry a pistol onto a plane. Already on probation in Providence for assaulting a college teammate with a tire iron, Barnes was sentenced to a year in prison for violating the terms of his probation.

Barnes was so far out his constant complaints hardly merited much attention, but the contention in the backcourt kept the Pistons in constant turmoil.

Kevin Porter, who was traded to Detroit in exchange for Dave Bing and then was injured after only 19 games in 1975, was the unhappiest of the group. Porter twice was fined by Brown and the two nearly came to blows. Porter had been slow recovering from his knee surgery of the previous season, so Money took over the play-making responsibility. Then Money got hurt and Porter returned to the lineup. It was when both were healthy that the real trouble started.

Ford and Simpson shared the other guard position, which did not sit well with Simpson, who claimed he okayed his trade from Denver to Detroit after the Pistons promised him a starting berth. Ford averaged 12.3 points, Simpson 11.0, Money 10.2 and Porter 8.9.

"We may gripe on the sidelines, but we perform on the court," Money said. "What's wrong with that? That's human. The Oakland A's won the World Series that way."

"Most of our players have no-cut multi-year contracts. Why they can't be happy in winning whether they make a contribution or not is beyond me," said Detroit General Manager Oscar Feldman.

The Pistons showed the good sense not to take any guards among their top draft choices, but if Central Michigan center Ben Poquette and Hofstra center-forward John Irving, the nation's No. 2 college rebounder, become starters, the Piston front line veterans will work up the courage to make their discontent known.

Nonetheless, the Pistons desperately needed Poquette or Irving or Iowa's Bruce King to come through with rebounding help. Despite the presence of man mountain Lanier, the Pistons were the third worst rebounding team in the league last season.

Irving's forte is rebounding as he lost the nation's rebounding title to Seton Hall's Glenn Mosley by only .01 last season in helping lead Hofstra into the NCAA tournament. Irving had a rebounding average of 16.30.

Drastic improvement defensively and in rebounding is a must for the Pistons to fulfill their championship potential, but the primary problem to be solved is one of maturity.

Statistics for 1976-77 season

Career statistics, not including those of the 1976-77 season

Player's name / Years in NBA prior to 1976-77	G	M	FGM	FTM	PTS	AVG	FG%	REB	ASST
Barnes, Marvin †(2 years)	53	989	202	106	510	9.6	.447	253	45
Carr, M.L. †(1 year)	144	5563	1458	546	3465	24.1	.501	1927	399
Douglas, Leon	82	2643	443	205	1091	13.3	.476	631	181
	74	2174	380	137	906	12.2	.487	459	224
	82	1626	245	127	617	7.5	.479	526	68
Eberhard, Al (2 years)	68	1219	181	109	471	6.9	.476	221	50
Ford, Chris (4 years)	115	2343	314	208	836	7.3	.409	437	99
Lanier, Bob (6 years)	82	2539	437	131	1005	12.3	.476	270	337
	318	7756	979	263	2221	7.0	.451	1130	975
	64	2446	678	260	1616	25.3	.534	745	214
	464	16,656	4168	1939	10,275	22.1	.497	5736	1564
Money, Eric (2 years)	73	1586	529	90	748	10.2	.521	124	243
Porter, Howard (5 years)	146	3156	593	176	1362	9.3	.468	295	439
Porter, Kevin (4 years)	78	2200	465	103	1033	13.2	.483	458	53
	316	5011	1064	317	2440	7.7	.458	1135	116
	81	2117	310	97	717	8.9	.512	98	592
Sellers, Phil	252	6832	1187	415	2789	11.1	.473	447	1549
	44	329	73	52	198	4.5	.384	41	25
Simpson, Ralph †(6 years)	77	1597	356	138	850	11.0	.427	181	180
	487	15,643	4022	1877	9953	20.4	.464	2171	1878

†—ABA totals

Most Promising Rookies: Ben Poquette, John Irving, Bruce King. The Pistons, wisely figuring they had more than enough depth at guard, went for big men in the college draft. Poquette, from unheralded Central Michigan, was a surprise pick and the big center will have strong competition from his more renowned rivals, Irving and King, for a spot on the Pistons' roster. Irving led Hofstra into the NCAA tournament last season as the No. 2 rebounder in the nation. He averaged 16.30 rebounds a game to barely lose the national rebounding title to Seton Hall's Glenn Mosley, who had an average of 16.31. King, the mainstay of Iowa's team for three years, was among the nation's leaders in scoring and rebounding. He averaged 21 points and 13.3 rebounds a game.

PERFORMANCE QUOTIENTS

Offense: Scoring is not one of the Pistons' problems. Detroit was sixth in the league in scoring and second in field goal percentage. Naturally, the offense revolves around center Lanier, who was the NBA's sixth leading scorer last season with a 25.3 average. He sank 53 per cent of his shots from the floor and 82 per cent from the foul line. The Pistons' wealth of guards is almost embarrassing. Money and Porter are considered the playmakers, while Ford and Simpson are regarded as the scorers. Porter was fourth in the league in assists with an average of 7.3. Actually, though, Ford was second on the Pistons in assists and Money shot an outstanding 52 per cent from the floor. All the guards do several things well. Although Barnes failed to live up to expectations because of his extracurricular activities, the potential still is there and he could be one of the best offensive forwards in the NBA. Regardless of what happens to Barnes, Carr has proved a capable performer in the NBA and averaged 13.3 points a game with a shooting percentage of .476. And Howard Porter had the best year of his career, averaging 13.2 points a game as the other shooting forward. **Perf. Qt.: 2.**

Defense: When it came to giving up points, only San Antonio and Milwaukee yielded more than the Pistons. The Pistons' defensive inadequacies completely negated their high-scoring offense. Lanier is no defensive wizard, but is so immense he does an adequate job against opposing centers merely by leaning on them a bit. Carr and H. Porter, though, leave the Pistons lacking defensively at the forward position. Ford is the best defensive performer among the guards, while Simpson probably is the weakest. **Perf. Qt.: 4.**

Rebounding: It's embarrassing for a team with Lanier to have the third lowest rebound total in the NBA. But Irving should help out here. **Perf. Qt.: 4.**

Midwest Division

Kansas City Kings

Prediction: Fourth

When you're holding a full hand of kings, it's almost always a safe bet to stand pat. Every once in a while, though, it helps to have an ace in the hole.

Such was the sad lesson learned last season by the Kansas City Kings, so set in their lineup that they were the only team in the NBA to go through the entire campaign without making a single roster change.

With a well-balanced squad on which six players averaged in double figures, seven contributed 100 or more assists and eight came through with at least 200 rebounds, the Kings appeared well on their way to a playoff berth in the tough Midwest Division.

Then came injuries to two regulars, guard Brian Taylor and forward Bill Robinzine, and both were lost for the final three weeks. As a result, Kansas City lost nine of its last 10 games and missed out on a playoff berth for the second consecutive year.

"I'm not sorry we didn't get into the playoffs," was the frank appraisal of General Manager Joe Axelson. "We wouldn't have been a good representative anyway."

Then, noting the failure to make any changes on the roster that started the campaign, Axelson said, "Basketball is a nine man game. You've got to have the people. We have some decent guards, but we didn't have the guys who could come off the bench in the final minute and go one-on-one when you needed a basket.

"I don't like trades. I don't think they can help you much. I don't like to shuffle bodies for the sake of shuffling bodies. If you have a player and I have a player of equal caliber, what sense would a trade make? If a guy hustles and works for me all year, I'm not going to trade him for someone of equal value. It would be unfair to him."

Axelson admitted, however, "We've got to strengthen our team and get more NBA starter-caliber players."

And that's when the pat hand was scattered to the wind and the kings began to fall.

The key departure was Taylor, who along with another ABA refugee, Ron Boone, gave Kansas City as strong a starting backcourt as there was in the NBA. Boone and Taylor were 1-2 in team scoring with averages of 22.2 and 17.0 respectively, and they ranked 2-3 in assists with 338 and 320 respectively.

But Taylor demanded to be traded, and the Kings accommodated him by sending him to Denver for 7-2 center Tom Burleson, whom the Nuggets had acquired that same day from Seattle.

Shortly after that, KC got back a quality guard by obtaining Lucius Allen from Los Angeles for reserve forward Ollie Johnson plus the Kings' first and second round draft picks next year.

A third key addition came in the draft when Kansas City, with the second pick overall, chose All-America guard Otis Birdsong of Houston.

The addition of Birdsong, Allen and Burleson to a roster that already includes Boone, Scott Wedman,

Robinzine, Sam Lacey and Richard Washington provides Kansas City fans with hope for a happier ending this season.

Birdsong was the nation's highest scoring senior last year, averaging a hefty 30.3 points per game, and he ranks second only behind Elvin Hayes in career scoring at Houston. He'll go into his rookie campaign as the No. 3 guard behind Boone and Allen, according to Coach Phil Johnson, but he's certain to see heavy duty.

"Ron Boone and Lucius Allen are both proven guards and I know I can learn a lot from both of them," said the practical 6-4 Birdsong. "I'm happy to go with a team with a lot of young talent. When you have a lot of young talent, you can do a lot of things—like run."

Despite the personal tutelage of Bill Russell, Burleson never reached his potential in three years at Seattle. His scoring average fell off in each succeeding season, sinking to a low of 9.7 in 1976-77, and his 551 rebounds also marked a career low.

Still, at 25, Burleson represents a worthy gamble, and Axelson admitted that he has been interested in the giant center ever since his college days.

"Burleson is a force and, coupled with Sam Lacey, gives us two starting centers with complementing offensive and defensive skills that will enable Coach Phil Johnson to match up against just about anybody," Axelson said.

Allen, after playing out his option with Los Angeles, is returning to his hometown. He averaged 14.6 points for the Lakers last season, a fraction above his career average, and also had a team high 405 assists.

"Allen is the ideal running mate to complement Boone and Birdsong," said Johnson. "He has the ability to penetrate, score and run the club. His experience, quickness and court savvy will undoubtedly strengthen our backcourt for the coming years."

Boone, only an 11th-round draft pick of Phoenix back in 1968, opted instead for the ABA and he went on to become that league's third highest scorer in history (behind Lou Dampier and Dan Issel). In his eight years in the ABA, the 31-year-old guard didn't miss a game.

"I knew we were getting an outstanding player, but he's even better than I had anticipated," said Johnson of the prize he picked up in last summer's dispersal draft. "The only thing that concerned us was his age. But he plays young and he's in great physical shape. Not only has he never missed a game since high school, but he's never missed a practice."

The 6-10 Lacey and 6-11 Washington gave Kansas City good strength under the boards last season, grabbing 734 and 698 rebounds respectively. Lacey, a center, expressed unhappiness at one point in the campaign with his role on offense. "I'm nothing but a passer," he said. "There's no plays for me. Not one. I guess Phil feels I don't need to be involved in the offense."

Lacey had only a 12.8 career average for his first six years, and last season fell to 10.6.

Washington, used at both center and forward, broke into the pros with a 13-point average and had 90 blocked shots to Lacey's 133.

"Richard has certainly lived up to expectations, and then some," said Johnson. "He's a very relaxed performer, almost a gentle giant. If he keeps his intensity, I don't see how he can help but be great."

PREDICTION: FOURTH

Statistics for 1976-77 season

Career statistics, not including those of the 1976-77 season

Player's name / Years in NBA prior to 1976-77	G	M	FGM	FTM	PTS	AVG	FG%	REB	ASST
*Allen, Lucius (7 years)	78	2482	472	195	1139	14.6	.456	251	405
Barr, Mike (7 years)	516	15,117	2970	1251	7191	13.9	.469	1679	2365
†(4 years)	73	1224	122	41	285	3.9	.437	130	175
Boone, Ron	234	5117	631	248	1519	6.5	.492	502	686
†(8 years)	82	3021	747	324	1818	22.2	.474	321	338
**Burleson, Tom	662	21,586	4695	2640	12,153	18.4	.472	3302	2569
(2 years)	82	1803	288	220	796	9.7	.442	551	93
Eakins, Jim	164	4535	818	473	2109	12.9	.453	1314	295
†(8 years)	82	1338	151	188	490	6.0	.449	361	119
Lacey, Sam	652	17,279	2705	2217	7627	11.7	.508	5142	1197
(6 years)	82	2595	327	215	869	10.6	.422	734	386
McCarter, Andre	482	17,978	2616	947	6179	12.8	.436	6042	1584
	59	725	119	32	270	4.6	.463	55	99
Robinzine, Bill (1 year)	75	1594	307	159	773	10.3	.453	474	95
Washington, Richard	75	1327	229	145	603	8.0	.459	355	60
	82	2265	446	177	1069	13.0	.431	698	85
Wedman, Scott	81	2743	521	206	1248	15.4	.460	506	227
(2 years)	162	5522	913	330	2156	13.3	.459	1096	328

*—Acquired from Los Angeles
**—Seattle totals; acquired from Denver
†—ABA totals

Most Promising Rookies: Otis Birdsong, Eddie Owens. With the second pick in the draft, Kansas City plucked itself a prize in Birdsong, a 30.3 scorer in his final year at Houston. The 6-4 guard hit on a phenomenal 56.9 per cent of his floor shots to move into second place behind Elvin Hayes on the all-time scoring list at Houston. Birdsong will break in as the No. 3 guard, to which he said, "Ron Boone and Lucius Allen are both proven guards and I know I can learn a lot from both of them. I'm happy to be with a team with a lot of young talent. When you have this young talent you can do a lot of things, like run." Owens, a 6-6 forward, averaged 21.8 points last season at the University of Nevada-Las Vegas.

PERFORMANCE QUOTIENTS

Offense: The Kings had one of the most explosive backcourts in the business last season in Boone and Brian Taylor, both ABA refugees, with averages of 22.2 and 17.0, respectively. But at his own request, Taylor, who hit on better than 50 per cent of his floor shots, was traded away. However, Kansas City more than compensated for Taylor's loss by acquiring Allen, another veteran guard, and drafting Otis Birdsong. Allen averaged 14.6 points for Los Angeles last season, and KC Coach Phil Johnson says "he'll give us the ideal running mate to complement Boone and Birdsong. He has the ability to penetrate, score and run a club." Burleson, another new acquisition, has yet to prove himself a consistent scorer, but at 25 the 7-2 center still has the potential. Wedman, Washington, Lacey and Robinzine hit in double figures last year, presenting the possibility of Kansas City putting together a powerful attack. **Perf. Qt.: 3.**

Defense: With Lacey and Burleson clogging up the middle, the Kings should also be improved in this important department after allowing 106.8 points last year. Lacey is very strong defensively, blocking 133 shots last season and making 119 steals. Burleson was almost as impressive with 117 blocked shots and 74 steals for Seattle. Allen is a crafty veteran and will help settle the backcourt. **Perf. Qt.: 3.**

Rebounding: With Burleson joining Lacey and Washington, Kansas City can prove awesome under the boards. Lacey grabbed 734 rebounds last season, Washington had 698 and Burleson, with far less playing time, had 551. In addition, Wedman had 506 rebounds and Robinzine 474. One of the reasons Lacey is so effective under the boards is his willingness to sacrifice points to concentrate on other essentials. As he put it, "Some guys let their offense dictate the way the rest of their game is going to go. They have to realize how important it is to do other things. When I'm not shooting well or getting a lot of shots, I try to concentrate on things like rebounding or defense." **Perf. Qt.: 2.**

Midwest Division

Milwaukee Bucks

Prediction: Fifth

You don't need a degree in trivia to recollect the circumstances the last time the Milwaukee Bucks won a coin toss that gave them the No. 1 pick in the collegiate draft. That was back in 1969 when they chose a towering, skinny center from NCAA champion UCLA named Lew Alcindor.

Two years later, just about the time he was formally adopting his new name, Kareem Abdul-Jabbar led the Bucks to the NBA championship.

That, of course, is so much history now, albeit an important piece of basketball lore. Milwaukee enjoyed several good years, although falling far short of the dynasty that some were predicting, and Abdul-Jabbar eventually took his talents back to Los Angeles.

The nostalgia of this fairly formidable success story, of a rags-to-riches expansion team, came to mind last spring when the Bucks once again won the coin toss. And once more they gambled their fortune on a center who had guided his college team to an NCAA championship.

At 6-11, Kent Benson is some 3-4 inches shorter than Lew Alcindor was, but he is a good deal broader. No one in the Milwaukee organization is really comparing him to Abdul-Jabbar yet, and there isn't wild talk of this baby giant showing the way back to the top.

But make no mistake, the pressure is there. As if being No. 1 isn't enough, the Bucks squeezed the noose ever so much tighter by trading away last year's regular center, Swen Nater. In ever so polite a way, they've told Kent Benson that he's expected right from the start to fill the most crucial position on a basketball team.

Don Nelson, starting his first full season as coach, concedes that Benson isn't likely to become another Abdul-Jabbar, but added, "He can be a dominating player in his own way. Benson isn't a shot-blocker, but in our kind of defense it's not so important to block shots as it is to play position."

Benson injured his back in a fall last year, causing him to miss the last four games of his career at Indiana. Still, he was selected to the All-America team for a second consecutive time after averaging 19.8 points per game with 241 rebounds in 23 outings. He has a good hook shot and jumper and enjoys physical contact.

Benson, who also made the All-America Academic team two years, reported during the summer that his back is recovered fully. He will be the beneficiary of welcome help with Milwaukee in the presence of guard Quinn Buckner, a teammate on Indiana's 1976 championship team.

The excitement emanating from training camp had to do with more than the presence of Benson. In what amounted to a coup of sorts, Milwaukee also had the third and 11th choices in the first round of the draft, selecting a pair of offensive-minded forwards, 6-7 Marques Johnson of UCLA, who was named as College Player of the Year, and 6-5 Ernie Grunfeld of Tennessee.

Johnson is the highest scoring forward in UCLA history and also ranks among the school's top five career performers in scoring and rebounding. His figures last season were 21.5 points and 10.7 rebounds. Grunfeld, who averaged 22.8 points last season, also plays guard and was a teammate of Buckner on the 1976 Olympic gold medalists.

"I think we just got the best draft in the history of the NBA," stated James FitzGerald, president of the Bucks. To which Nelson added, "I would say there is a possibility all three of them could start for us this year."

On the second and third rounds, Milwaukee drafted a pair of 6-4 guards, Glen Williams of St. John's, a 21.5 scorer last season, and Gary Yoder of Cincinnati, who scored at a 13.6 pace. This prompted General Manager Bob Ferry of the Washington Bullets to comment, "They drafted a starting lineup. They had five picks in the first 47 and they got a great center, two great forwards, a shooting guard and a playmaker. It's overwhelming."

So, to say that the Bucks will present a new look this season is a shallow understatement. This would particularly be the case if forward Bob Dandridge followed through with his threat to leave Milwaukee after playing out his option.

Ironically, Dandridge was drafted by Milwaukee the same year as Alcindor, in the fourth round, and was the last survivor of the 1971 championship team. He led the Bucks in scoring last season with a 20.8 average and was runnerup in rebounding (440) and third in assists (268).

Except for Dandridge and Nater, who is now gone, only two other Milwaukee players hit in double figures last season. Guard Brian Winters and swingman Junior

Bridgeman, both of whom were acquired in the monumental Abdul-Jabbar deal of two years ago, averaged 19.3 and 14.4 points respectively.

The problem with Winters, who also contributed 440 rebounds and 268 assists, is that he goes through too many cold spells. "I may shoot real well in warmups and then not be able to hit anything in the game," says the 25-year-old, 6-4 graduate of South Carolina. "Then again, I might not be able to hit anything in warmups and then have a hot hand in the game. It just sort of comes and goes."

Part of the reason for Milwaukee's dismal showing last season was surgery on Dave Meyers during the summer of 1976. As a result, the 6-9, 225-pound forward, counted on heavily by the Bucks, played in only 50 games and had a disappointing 9.7 average with only 341 rebounds.

Another man who should contribute a lot more this season is Buckner. Not that the 6-3 guard didn't produce in his rookie campaign, when he won a starting berth and functioned as the floor leader, but now he's NBA wise and he should have the kind of troops who can better take advantage of his unselfish play.

Buckner averaged 8.6 points last season and led the team in assists with 372. He found it distasteful, though, being part of such a poor team after winning the NCAA championship the previous year. "I know how to take losing, but I don't accept it. I never will accept it and I'll always strive to get us winning again."

This is the season it should start. Certainly, the Bucks will improve on their 30-52 record, the second worst in the NBA, although the rise to the top isn't likely to be as fast as it was after Lew Alcindor was drafted in 1969.

Player's name / Statistics for 1976-77 season

Career statistics, not including those of the 1976-77 season

Years in NBA prior to 1976-77	G	M	FGM	FTM	PTS	AVG	FG%	REB	ASST
Bridgeman, Junior (1 year)	82	2410	491	197	1179	14.4	.449	416	205
Buckner, Quinn	81	1646	286	128	700	8.6	.439	294	157
	79	2095	299	83	681	8.6	.434	264	372
*Carter, Fred (7 years)	61	1112	209	68	486	8.0	.418	117	125
	550	17,216	3708	1369	8785	16.0	.425	2264	1997
Dandridge, Bob (7 years)	70	2501	585	283	1453	20.8	.467	440	268
	537	19,419	4220	1533	9973	18.6	.491	4040	1675
English, Alex	60	648	132	45	310	5.2	.477	168	25
**Garrett, Rowland (4 years)	62	598	106	41	253	4.1	.444	112	27
	201	2307	456	172	1084	5.4	.441	495	79
Lloyd, Scott	69	1025	153	95	401	5.8	.472	210	33
Meyers, Dave (1 year)	50	1262	179	127	485	9.7	.467	341	86
	72	1589	198	135	531	7.4	.419	445	100
Restani, Kevin (2 years)	64	1116	173	12	358	5.6	.518	262	88
	158	3405	422	59	903	5.7	.459	779	215
Walton, Lloyd	53	678	88	53	229	4.3	.468	51	141
Winters, Brian (2 years)	78	2717	652	205	1509	19.3	.498	231	337
	146	4311	977	256	2210	15.1	.456	387	561

*—Combined Philadelphia-Milwaukee totals
**—Combined Cleveland-Milwaukee totals

PREDICTION: FIFTH

Most Promising Rookies: Kent Benson, Marques Johnson, Ernie Grunfeld, Glen Williams, Gary Yoder. In what isn't much of an exaggeration, Bucks' President James Fitzgerald claimed, "I think we just got the best draft in the history of the NBA." Benson, a 6-11, 245-pound center, was a two-time All-America who improved his scoring figures each year at Indiana, reaching a peak of 19.8 points as a senior. He's a strong rebounder with a good hook shot and a 15-foot jumper who says he'd like to pattern himself after Dave Cowens. Johnson, a 6-7, 215-pound forward, was selected College Player of the Year as a senior when he averaged 21.5 points and 10.7 rebounds, and he is the highest scoring forward in UCLA history. Grunfeld, a 6-5 swingman, averaged 22.8 points at Tennessee last season; Williams, a 6-4 guard, scored at a 21.5 point clip for St. John's; and Yoder, also a 6-4 guard, averaged 13.6 points at Cincinnati.

PERFORMANCE QUOTIENTS

Offense: The Milwaukee offense was adequate last season, averaging 108.4 points, but the bucket may go up in smoke this year with all the new artillery that has been added. With three of the first 15 choices in the collegiate draft, the Bucks virtually turned their starting lineup around with the additions of Kent Benson, Marques Johnson and Ernie Grunfeld. Benson isn't an explosive scorer, having averaged 19.8 points in his senior year at Indiana. He has a good hook shot and is deadly with a 15-foot jumper, and in each of his four campaigns in school he hit on better than 50 per cent of his floor shots, including a .578 mark as a junior. Johnson, a 21.5 scorer last season, is the highest scoring forward in UCLA history and Grunfeld, with a range of up to 20 feet, averaged 22.8 points last season. They will add a lot of punch to a team that already had a 20-point scorer in Dandridge and a 19-point scorer in Winters. More offensive help can be anticipated from Meyers, a former teammate of Johnson at UCLA who was slow recovering from knee surgery a year ago. **Perf. Qt.: 3.**

Defense: Milwaukee had the second most porous defense last season, yielding 111.5 points, as good a reason as any why the Bucks failed to qualify for the playoffs. Benson, an aggressive defender, has to be an improvement on a team that had no intimidating capability. An indication is that the team leader in blocked shots was Elmore Smith with 69, and he played in only 34 games before being traded. Buckner, though, was fourth in the NBA in steals with 192 and he can provide leadership with experience. **Perf. Qt.: 5.**

Rebounding: Swen Nater, since dealt away, was the team leader with 865, and after him Dandridge's 440 rebounds was the next best. Obviously, a lot of help is needed, and just how much Benson and Johnson can provide as rookies has yet to be seen. **Perf. Qt.: 4.**

Midwest Division

Indiana Pacers

Prediction: Sixth

When the Indiana Pacers play their first game of the season, they will have scored the biggest victory of their 10-year history. And that will take place before the game even starts.

Forget the three championships the Pacers won in the ABA, and never mind that they had a playoff contender in each of their nine years in the old league. None of that can hold a candle to survival itself, and that's exactly what the club was fighting for during the long spring and summer.

Bobby Leonard, the team's coach and general manager, called it "a three-week sudden death overtime." The object of the game was to sell 8,000 ticket sales to help meet the payroll and keep the franchise alive. A Fourth of July telethon enabled them to reach that goal.

The Pacers weren't too fortunate on the court in their maiden NBA season, although they certainly did better than some skeptics predicted. After playing .500 ball for the first half of the season, they wound up 36-46, finishing fifth in the six-team Midwest Division and missing out on the playoffs for the first time in club history.

"I feel we could have won 40 or so, but even that's not good enough," Leonard said. "Obviously, we've got to strengthen ourselves. We beat out six clubs, but didn't get into the playoffs and that's our goal."

As for the second half slide, after the Pacers compiled a 21-20 record, Leonard said, "I just feel we weren't mentally tough enough during the second half. Eighty, almost 90 per cent of the time when I went to my bench, I got hurt. Obviously, that bench has to be strengthened."

That strength that Leonard needs can best be supplied by physicians. Center Len Elmore, a fearsome rebounder, played only 46 minutes during the entire season because of a knee injury and Dan Roundfield, who replaced Elmore in the pivot, was lost for the last couple of months with a sprained right ankle. If these two young men return healthy, they will provide a tremendous boost.

Leonard was hoping to obtain a big center, employing Elmore as his backup and moving Roundfield, who is only 6-8, to forward. "And if we can't get that big guy to play inside," he added, "we have to try to surround people like Dave Robisch [another center] and Elmore with more talented players."

The Pacers weren't able to get immediate help in the draft. As part of the deal that brought them John Williamson from the Nets, they dealt away their first-round choice. In the second round they took 6-6 forward Alonzo Bradley of Texas Southern.

Billy Knight, only a third-year pro, achieved instant stardom in the NBA as he placed second in the league scoring race behind Kareem Abdul-Jabbar with a 26.6 average. A slick, versatile performer, called "Mr. Smooth" by his teammates, the 6-6 Knight played both guard and forward, was selected to play in the All-Star game, and was second on the team in both assists (260) and steals (117) and third in rebounds (582).

Wherever he plays, Knight takes particular pride in his rebounding. "I'm not really that physically strong," he said, "but I like to go to the boards, particularly on the offensive end of the floor. I'm just an average jumper, but I rebound well because I use my head and can be sneaky going after the ball."

Atlanta Coach Hubie Brown was impressed enough to say of Knight, "He's better than David Thompson. He's a super player and an All-Star performer." Brown may have been biased in his feelings after watching Knight hit for 41 points against his team.

At the other end of the court, Indiana has the best defensive guard in the game in Don Buse. The 6-4 Evansville alumnus is another of those former ABA players who were almost unknown by rivals and fans alike in the NBA, despite the fact that in the ABA's final year of existence he set league records for both steals and assists.

The changeover in leagues didn't bother Buse's style, as he again won the twin titles, compiling 685 assists and 281 steals. Only one other player, Slick Watts of Seattle with 214, had as many as 200 steals.

"I'm not as quick as Watts or Walt Frazier," Buse said of his knack for stealing balls. "But I do have exceptionally quick hands."

At a banquet prior to the NBA All-Star game, in which he played, Buse joked that he became a good passer when the Indiana front court consisted of Knight and George McGinnis. "They said to me, 'Listen, you're going to have to learn to do something besides shoot, because we're going to do all the shooting around here.'"

Particularly when Knight is at guard, the Pacers

virtually have a one-guard, four-forward offense with Buse handling the ball almost 90 per cent of the time. "He complements me so well," Knight said. "It's like I was still playing forward because on offense I can do the exact same things."

There is a sharp difference of opinion on how wise the Pacers were in making the deal for Williamson. True, the 6-2 guard averaged 20.7 points in 30 games for Indiana, but he cost them the sixth choice overall in the college draft plus 6-9 Darnell Hillman, the "player to be named later," who led Indiana in rebounding with 693, was second in blocked shots with 106 and turned in a respectable 10.7 scoring average.

"We needed more punch, and getting Williamson allowed us to move Knight back to forward," Leonard explained. "We feel that John is a far better player than anyone we would have been able to get in the draft."

It is not so coincidental that Indiana's slide started after Roundfield was injured. The Pacers won only four of their next 14 games even though his replacement, Robisch, averaged 18.4 points for those 18 contests.

"I think Danny has improved at least as much as anybody in the league," Leonard said of Roundfield, who started out the campaign as his No. 3 center. "He's much more competitive than he was as a rookie the year before—he's finding out what this game is all about. He jumps like a player who is 6-foot-10 or better."

Roundfield, who said he worked on his jump shot all through the summer of 1976, improving it 30-40 per cent, averaged 13.9 points, led the team in blocked shots with 131 and had 518 rebounds.

PREDICTION: SIXTH

Statistics for 1976-77 season

Career statistics, not including those of the 1976-77 season

Player's name / Years in NBA prior to 1976-77	G	M	FGM	FTM	PTS	AVG	FG%	REB	ASST
Anderson, Jerome (1 year)	27	164	26	14	66	2.4	.441	12	10
Bennett, Mel †(1 year)	22	126	25	11	61	2.8	.556	13	6
Buse, Don	67	911	101	112	314	4.7	.344	237	70
†(1 year)	75	2193	329	246	904	12.1	.403	526	97
†(4 years)	81	2947	266	114	646	8.0	.416	270	685
Elmore, Len	318	9107	949	356	2405	7.6	.466	1058	1505
†(2 years)	6	46	7	4	18	3.0	.412	15	2
Flynn, Mike †(1 year)	153	4005	698	224	1621	10.6	.407	1214	157
	73	1324	250	101	601	8.2	.436	187	179
Green, Steve †(1 year)	67	1097	166	64	421	6.3	.415	133	133
	70	918	183	84	450	6.4	.432	177	46
Jones, Wil	52	1068	195	84	474	9.1	.450	194	64
†(7 years)	80	2709	438	166	1042	13.0	.430	604	189
Knight, Billy	566	17,511	2878	1138	6906	12.2	.470	4622	1141
†(2 years)	78	3117	831	413	2075	26.6	.493	582	260
Robisch, Dave	150	5334	1354	622	3340	22.3	.512	1340	427
†(5 years)	80	1966	369	213	951	11.9	.455	554	158
Roundfield, Dan †(1 year)	422	12,224	2303	1549	6155	14.6	.470	3553	842
	61	1645	342	164	848	13.9	.466	518	69
*Williamson, John †(3 years)	67	767	131	77	339	5.1	.427	259	35
	72	2481	618	259	1495	20.8	.459	193	201
	228	6391	1371	460	3215	14.1	.479	552	628

†—ABA totals

*—Combined Nets-Indiana totals

INDIANA PACERS

Most Promising Rookie: Alonzo Bradley. The Pacers, although badly needing help, didn't get to choose in the first round of the draft and when their turn finally came around in the second they chose Bradley, a 6-6 forward from Texas Southern. In 68 games during his two-year career at Texas Southern, Bradley averaged 24.7 points with a total of 553 rebounds and 198 assists. He had a fine field goal percentage of 56.2. One Indiana official called Bradley a Billy Knight type, and added, "Hopefully, he'll give us a small forward coming off the bench, which is something we didn't have before."

PERFORMANCE QUOTIENTS

Offense: After struggling through the summer months in a fight for survival, the Pacers may not feel it was worth coming back for another campaign unless they can find some scoring strength. Except for Knight, who quickly established himself as one of the best pure shooters in the NBA, and newcomer Williamson, no one averaged as much as 14 points a game last season. Indiana's shooting percentage of .449 was the third lowest in the NBA and even though Williamson averaged 20.8 points for the season, his field goal percentage of .459 shows that he did a lot of shooting. Knight, equally effective whether he is used at forward or guard, ranked second in the league scoring race with a 26.6 average, more than four points better than his two-year figures in the ABA. Says Mr. Smooth, "I don't consider myself a streak shooter since I'm over 50 per cent for my career, but I do have streaks when everything I throw up there goes in." Roundfield, an immensely improved player from his rookie campaign, when he averaged only 5.1 points in the ABA, was a 13.9 scorer and Jones was at 13. But Indiana is going to need a lot more help. **Perf. Qt.: 4.**

Defense: The lack of a big man to clog up the middle is going to cost the Pacers dearly again. Roundfield, at 6-8 the shortest center in the NBA last season, was credited with 131 blocked shots in 61 games, but if Indiana has to go with him again at center, it will be difficult to intimidate rival shooters. The Pacers allowed 108.6 points last season, the fifth most porous defense in the league. Len Elmore, sidelined by injury last season, blocked 178 shots and had 136 steals in 1975-76, and his return would provide a great boost. **Perf. Qt.: 4.**

Rebounding: Once again, the return of Elmore, a tenacious rebounder, is the key element here. Although the Pacers lacked one dominant man on the boards, they did fairly well as a team with five men notching 500 or more rebounds. The leaders were Darnell Hillman (since sent to the Nets) with 693 and Jones with 604. Even from the guard position, Knight concentrates on rebounding and brought down 582 last season. **Perf. Qt.: 3.**

Pacific Division

Portland Trail Blazers

Prediction: First

It is one thing when a corporate executive wins a million dollar lottery. It is another matter indeed when the lucky ticket holder is a down-and-out laborer with a roomful of unpaid bills.

Let the Boston Celtics win the NBA championship, and before the fans have even exited from the Garden they'll be muttering, "Yeah, but the Red Sox look lousy this year." But when the Portland Trail Blazers come away with the crown, it is time for citywide celebrating.

And this is just what took place that Sunday afternoon, June 5, moments after Portland had won the final game of the championship series from the Philadelphia 76ers. There was mass bedlam throughout Portland with thousands and thousands of people swigging champagne and beer as they lined Broadway, filled up the Rose Festival's carnival along the Willamette River and waved banners.

The party carried over until the next afternoon, which was proclaimed Portland Trail Blazers day. The team was given a parade through downtown Portland and a presentation at City Hall. Said Mayor Neil Goldschmidt, "The Trail Blazers are Portland's team, the championship is Portland's championship, and this is a way for all of us to show our appreciation for the best basketball team in the world, on the court and off."

The "best basketball team in the world" had finished in the Pacific Division cellar five of the previous six years, had never before been in the playoffs and never in its history had so much as turned in a winning record. And this is why sports, with all its uncertainty and unpredictability, is such a turn-on and why Portland's championship is the best thing that could have happened to basketball.

Because the Trail Blazers never before had a good team, and because they had no other name stars besides Bill Walton, there is a tendency to dismiss their championship as a fluke. But make no mistake about it, as long as Walton remains relatively healthy, Portland has a strong, well-balanced club with the kind of speed and team presence that will win a lot of games.

"Portland is a great team," Los Angeles Coach Jerry West said after his Lakers were wiped out in four games in the playoff semifinals. "It has as fine personnel as there is in basketball. There is great depth in the backcourt. It is a team that is going to be good for a long time."

Coach Jack Ramsay, who has a doctorate in physical education, came to Portland a year ago after four seasons at Buffalo, and found the kind of team "I have long yearned to coach. We have the ideal center in Bill Walton, a powerful forward in Maurice Lucas and swift guards in Dave Twardzik, Lionel Hollins and Johnny Davis."

The winning formula is simple: Walton and Lucas control the defensive boards and throw an outlet pass to one of the speeding guards, who often is clear for an uncontested layup. This simple play provided the winning points in enough games to build a championship.

Unquestionably, the Trail Blazers revolve around Walton. After being limited to 86 games in his first two years because of injuries, the 6-11 center played in 65 last season. He led the league in rebounding with a 14.4 average and in blocked shots with 3.25 a game, while averaging 18.6 points.

But in assessing Walton's contributions, you must look beyond statistics. He is the team leader and inspiration, or, as Ramsay put it, "our team captain in every sense of the word. There is no better player, no more cooperative player, no better person than Bill."

There were two key acquisitions from the ABA before last season, Lucas, a powerful 6-9 forward, and Twardzik, an intense, 6-1 guard. Both earned starting jobs and were close to being indispensable.

Lucas earned a reputation in the ABA as an intimidator after decking 7-2 Artis Gilmore, and he showed a national television audience how tough he can be by going after Philadelphia's Darryl Dawkins during the finals. But Lucas is far more than mere threat. He led Portland in scoring last season with a 20.2 average, ranked ninth in the NBA in rebounding with an 11.4 average, and even had 229 assists and 83 steals.

"Eventually, Lucas and Walton will give us the best rebounding pair in the league," Ramsay stated. "Maurice has the ability to play the other team's big forward and his aggressive style fits our needs. He and Walton give us the opportunity to play a small forward at the other position, thereby increasing our running game which gets our offense going."

A bonus quality is that Lucas stood at only six feet

his first two years in high school, so he played guard and he is still able to handle the ball well.

Twardzik, with his blond hair and boyish smile, doesn't look like a professional basketball player—until he steps on the court. Then, to use his expression, he "plays like a kamikaze," diving all over for loose balls and generally wreaking havoc.

Twardzik, virtually unknown when he played for the Virginia Squires of the ABA, averaged 11.4 points per game, but he had a sensational field goal percentage of .612, far above Kareem Abdul-Jabbar's league best of .579. However, with only 263 field goals, Twardzik fell 37 shy of the minimum required to qualify for the statistical title.

Also averaging in double figures last season were Hollins (14.7), scrappy Bob Gross, the other regular forward (11.4), and swingman Larry Steele (10.3). Hollins also was the team leader in assists with 313 and steals with 166.

Portland had competent relief help up front last season with Lloyd Neal, a good rebounder who was limited to 58 games because of injury, Robin Jones, the only free agent rookie to make it in the NBA last year, rookie Wally Walker, who had a slow baptism after being drafted in the first round, and Corky Calhoun, a virtual walk-on.

In the draft, Portland had hoped to claim 6-11 center Jack Sikma as a backup for Walton, but when he was chosen by Seattle, the Blazers opted for 6-6 forward Rich Laurel of Hofstra, a 22.2 career scorer and a strong rebounder.

Unlike the old days—of a year or so ago—it no longer is easy to break into the Blazers' lineup. After all, they are the world champions.

PREDICTION: FIRST

Player's name — Statistics for 1976-77 season

Career statistics, not including those of the 1976-77 season

Years in NBA prior to 1976-77	G	M	FGM	FTM	PTS	AVG	FG%	REB	ASST
Calhoun, Corky (4 years)	70	743	85	66	236	3.4	.464	144	35
Davis, Johnny	305	7426	783	292	1858	6.1	.456	1355	375
Gilliam, Herm	79	1451	234	166	634	8.0	.441	126	148
(6 years)	80	1665	326	92	744	9.3	.438	201	170
Gross, Bob	498	13,361	2370	768	5508	11.1	.441	1974	2055
(1 year)	82	2232	376	183	935	11.4	.529	394	242
Hollins, Lionel	76	1474	209	97	515	6.8	.523	307	163
(1 year)	76	2224	452	215	1119	14.7	.432	210	313
Jones, Robin	74	1891	311	178	800	10.8	.421	175	306
	63	1065	139	66	344	5.5	.465	296	80
Lucas, Maurice	79	2863	632	335	1599	20.2	.466	899	229
†(2 years)	166	5325	1058	397	2518	15.2	.467	1786	511
Neal, Lloyd	58	955	160	77	397	6.8	.471	255	58
(4 years)	312	8838	1545	679	3769	12.1	.483	2733	492
Steele, Larry	81	1680	326	183	835	10.3	.500	188	172
(5 years)	376	10,031	1219	552	2990	8.0	.497	1264	1251
Twardzik, Dave	74	1937	263	239	765	10.3	.612	202	247
†(4 years)	256	6320	763	776	2311	9.0	.511	675	883
Walker, Wally	66	627	137	67	341	5.2	.449	108	51

	G	M	FGM	FTM	PTS	AVG	FG%	REB	ASST
Walton, Bill (2 years)	65	2264	491	228	1210	18.6	.528	899	229
†—ABA totals	86	2840	522	227	1271	14.8	.485	1122	387

Most Promising Rookies: Rich Laurel, Kim Anderson, T.R. Dunn. Laurel, playing at Hofstra, an unheralded New York school, was the fifth leading scorer in the country last season with a 30.3 average, and his career mark was 22.2. According to Stu Inman, director of player personnel for the world champions, "He's very agile and he might be able to see action as a guard. He's a good outside shooter, and he also can drive the basket." Anderson, a 6-8 forward, was a 14-point career scorer at Missouri and rebounds well, although Inman says, "He needs at least a year of patient handling and needs to add about 20 pounds." Dunn, a defense-oriented 6-4 guard from Alabama, isn't that good a ball-handler and Inman calls him "a gamble."

PERFORMANCE QUOTIENTS

Offense: You can forget the past book when it comes to picking apart the Trail Blazers, since they were reborn again in their championship season. It's a team concept stressed by Coach Jack Ramsay, and although they didn't have a single representative among the top 20 scorers in the league, the Blazers had six men in double figures and overall they were the third most explosive club with a 111.7 average. That's what's meant by a team concept. Lucas, playing his first year in the NBA, led the champions with a 20.2 average with Walton next at 18.6. Gross and Walton ranked sixth and eighth respectively in field goal percentage with marks of .529 and .528, while Twardzik shot at an incredible .612 pace, although he didn't qualify for the statistical title since he didn't take enough shots. **Perf. Qt.: 1.**

Defense: Here, too, the team concept is stressed as four players had more than 100 steals. Hollins, a tenacious guard, led the way with 166, followed by Twardzik with 128, Steele with 118 and Gross with 107. Walton was the league leader in blocked shots with a 3.25 average. The Blazers probably have the fastest team in basketball, an asset they put to advantage, with a clinging full-court press. **Perf. Qt.: 2.**

Rebounding: Ramsay feels that in time—perhaps this season—Walton and Lucas will give him the best rebounding pair in the game. He already may have that distinction inasmuch as Walton led the NBA last season with a 14.4 average and Lucas was ninth at 11.4. No other team was able to place two men among the top 10. **Perf. Qt.: 3.**

Pacific Division

Los Angeles Lakers

Prediction: Second

All Kareem Abdul-Jabbar needed was a great guard to set him up. After all, look at the championship won by the Milwaukee Bucks when Abdul-Jabbar teamed with Oscar Robertson.

Robertson's chief challenger for recognition as the best guard in basketball was Jerry West, so when Abdul-Jabbar was teamed with the former West Virginia great it should have been an inkling of things to come. However, West was joining the Los Angeles Lakers as head coach, not a playing guard, so it was not expected he could do a great deal to improve the team, which had been 40-42 the previous season.

But West turned the Lakers into a team centered around Abdul-Jabbar's incredible talents and everything was done to complement the big guy in the middle. As a result the Lakers won the Pacific Division regular season title with the best record in the National Basketball Association, 53-29.

And of course, Abdul-Jabbar cooperated by leading the NBA in field goal percentage, finishing second in rebounding and blocked shots and third in scoring. At the end of the season, Abdul-Jabbar won his fifth Most

Valuable Player Award, tying Bill Russell for the league record in hardware collection.

West received most of the credit for the Lakers' revival, but he quickly passed it on.

"I've always thought coaches probably got too much credit for winning and too much blame for losing," West said. "I've always been an optimist. When I took this job, I believed we could make the playoffs. But I didn't really believe something like this could happen.

"Basically, we have a collection of misfits no one else wanted. But they all have individual talents and they play well together.

"The players on this team have a very special kind of charisma for one another, an excellent chemistry."

Nonetheless, it is difficult to find any major difference in the Lakers other than West.

Abdul-Jabbar's outstanding season included a 26.2 scoring average, 1090 rebounds, a .579 field goal percentage and 319 assists. But the previous season, Abdul-Jabbar had a 27.7 scoring average, 1383 rebounds, a .529 shooting percentage and 413 assists, and still the Lakers wound up losers. His supporting cast was basically the same as the previous season.

So West and his assistant coaches, Stan Albeck and Jack McCloskey, must have had a great deal to do with the change in fortune.

West asked Lakers owner Jack Kent Cooke for permission to hire two assistants and the unusual troika proved a worthwhile investment.

"Since both of these people were obviously head coach types, I asked them if they could live with the kind of situation I had in mind and they said they could. It's worked out pretty well, even though we don't always agree. I can be pretty stubborn sometimes. The final decision on who plays and who doesn't has to be mine."

Albeck, who had been an assistant coach in the American Basketball Association, handles the Lakers' offense and McCloskey, the former coach of the Portland Trail Blazers, guides the defense.

It was on defense that the Lakers improved dramatically, finishing fourth in the league in fewest points allowed after being the second worst defensive team in the NBA the previous year.

"I'm happy again. Winning makes me happy," Abdul-Jabbar said. "It's what made Milwaukee tolerable. Last year we never got anything done. I was not optimistic in the preseason. But Jerry came in and organized, which I could not anticipate. Without arrogance, he was frank in what he wanted to do.

"You look at our team and you're not impressed. We got the type of players . . . well, people go to sleep on us."

But Kermit Washington, the nation's leading rebounder at American University and a big bust as the Lakers' No. 1 pick in 1973, suddenly emerged as the backboard helper Abdul-Jabbar needed, averaging 9.5 rebounds a game before being injured. His loss cost the Lakers dearly in their playoff series with Portland as Los Angeles had no one capable of offsetting Maurice Lucas.

The Lakers' No. 2 scorer last year was Cazzie Russell, but he may have been made expendable by Jamaal Wilkes, who, ironically, took the same free agent route down the California coast that Cazzie had followed three years ago. Wilkes averaged 17.7 points a game for the Golden State Warriors last season, to Russell's 16.4 for the Lakers. More significantly, he had almost twice as many rebounds, grabbing 578 despite his slender frame. And Wilkes is more than adequate on defense, a phase of the game Cazzie hasn't been able to master in 11 years as a pro.

The Lakers pursued free agent Wilkes at the urging of Jabbar, who preceded him at UCLA by a few years. Playing second fiddle to a big center will be nothing new for Jamaal, who played three years at Westwood in the shadow of Bill Walton. Another UCLA alumnus, Lucius Allen, was the Lakers' third leading scorer a year ago, but he has been traded to Kansas City. Allen averaged 14.6 points a game, and gave a lot of credit to former Boston Celtic star Don Chaney, who came back from knee surgery to become the defensive specialist the Lakers sorely needed.

"He takes most of the defensive pressure off me," Allen said. "Last year I had to play the big guards on the opposing teams and I must have been in foul trouble 40 different games. This year I've been in foul trouble about five times."

Earl Tatum, a 6-5 sharpshooter from Marquette, proved to be a valuable rookie for the Lakers with a 9.4 scoring average, and figures to be Allen's replacement.

And Abdul-Jabbar figures to get even more help next season as the Lakers had three first-round draft choices. North Carolina State forward Kenny Carr, a 6-7, 220-pounder, may be the Rookie of the Year as he seems perfectly suited for the Lakers.

"Kenny Carr may be the answer for our club," West said. "As far as talent, I don't think anyone in the draft has more."

The Lakers' other two first-round picks were guards Brad Davis, a hardship case like Carr, and Norm Nixon.

PREDICTION: SECOND

Player's name — Statistics for 1976-77 season

Career statistics, not including those of the 1976-77 season

Years in NBA prior to 1976-77	G	M	FGM	FTM	PTS	AVG	FG%	REB	ASST
Abdul-Jabbar, Kareem (7 years)	82	3016	888	376	2152	26.2	.579	1090	319
(7 years)	549	23,333	6816	2854	16,486	30.0	.545	8544	2421
Abernethy, Tom	70	1378	169	101	439	6.3	.484	291	98
Chaney, Don	81	2408	213	70	496	6.1	.408	330	308
(8 years)	485	12,566	1955	1013	4923	10.2	.450	2253	1106
Ford, Don	82	1782	202	73	597	7.3	.460	353	133
(1 year)	76	1838	311	104	726	6.5	.438	333	111
Kupec, C.J.	82	908	153	78	384	4.7	.447	199	53
(1 year)	16	55	10	7	87	10.9	.250	60	12
Lamar, Bo	71	1165	228	46	502	7.1	.406	92	177
(3 years)	202	6871	1630	598	3976	19.7	.429	647	886
Russell, Cazzie	82	2583	578	188	1344	16.4	.490	294	210
(10 years)	699	18,841	4461	1796	10,718	15.3	.471	2691	1567
Tatum, Earl	68	1249	283	72	638	9.4	.466	236	118
Warner, Cornell	14	170	25	4	52	3.9	.472	69	11
(6 years)	431	10,338	1165	476	2806	6.5	.452	3284	483
Washington, Kermit	53	1342	191	132	514	9.7	.503	492	48
(3 years)	136	1841	199	143	541	4.0	.444	662	105
Wilkes, Jamaal	76	2579	548	247	1343	17.7	.478	578	211
(2 years)	164	5231	1119	387	2625	16.0	.453	1391	350

Most Promising Rookies: Kenny Carr, Brad Davis, Norm Nixon. The Lakers had three picks in the first round of the college draft, so they made out like bandits. Carr is a 6-9 brute from North Carolina State capable of winning the Rookie of the Year Award. Not only should he be a perfect complement to Abdul-Jabbar under the backboards, but the youngster can also score. He averaged 21 points a game in his junior year before applying for the NBA draft as a hardship case. Davis, a 6-3 guard from Maryland, also went the hardship route after his junior season. He is a fine shooter, but he's known more for his flashy passes, though he sometimes misses connections with them. However, he should be a boost to the Lakers' fast break. Nixon averaged 22 points a game during his senior year at Duquesne and is a fine all-around backcourt man.

PERFORMANCE QUOTIENTS

Offense: The Lakers had the greatest offensive weapon in the league last season in Abdul-Jabbar. But this year they will be much better offensively. Abdul-Jabbar, the one player truly deserving of the label unstoppable, averaged 26.2 points a game by leading the league in field goal percentage with .579. He got some help last season from Russell and Allen, but, for the most part, was a one-man show. Things improved dramatically up front when the Lakers signed Wilkes as a free agent and drafted Kenny Carr. They'll put points on the scoreboard. Wilkes, who won the Rookie of the Year Award three seasons ago, averaged 17.7 points a game for the Warriors, connecting on 48 per cent of his shots. He also is a team-oriented player and had 211 assists. Tatum improved the Lakers' offense in his first season with tremendous outside shooting. He should get more playing time this year and increase on his 9.4 average. **Perf. Qt.: 2**

Defense: Abdul-Jabbar can be almost as imposing a force defensively as he is offensively. His tremendous shot-blocking ability (261 last season) makes up for a lot of mistakes by his teammates; consequently, they can gamble more on defense. The addition of Wilkes and the return of a physically fit Washington will strengthen the Lakers' front line defense. And, in Chaney, the Lakers have a top backcourt defender. **Perf. Qt.: 2**

Rebounding: Once again, Abdul-Jabbar is as good as there is. He pulled down more than 1000 last season and Washington proved an excellent complement before being injured. The lanky 6-7 Wilkes is a deceptively strong rebounder, finishing second in that department on the Warriors. Rookie Carr will add even more muscle underneath the boards, so the Lakers could be awesome in this department. **Perf. Qt.: 1.**

Pacific Division

Golden State Warriors

Prediction: Third

Rick Barry averaged 21.8 points a game, was sixth in the league in assists, ninth in steals and second in free throw percentage. Yet, Barry was a center of controversy on the Golden State Warriors.

The Warriors finished with a 46-36 record and extended the Los Angeles Lakers' Kareem Abdul-Jabbar to the height of his talents before being eliminated from the playoffs. But it was far from a successful season for the Warriors, who won the National Basketball Association championship two years ago.

Barry has little tolerance for anything less than excellence from his teammates and the outspoken forward criticized some of his teammates for not playing aggressively enough on defense and for not really being team-oriented.

"Look, I'm a perfectionist; I can never be satisfied," he said, discounting reports of dissension on the Warriors.

Barry is one of the most intelligent players in the game and cannot tolerate slovenly or stupid play from his teammates.

"People have this thing about scoring points," Barry said. "I was taught to play the game from a total concept, to be able to do everything reasonably well, some things extraordinarily well. If a guy is simply a great shooter and he has a bad night, he's a liability. If I'm not shooting well, I'll try to be an asset in other ways. So many players are limited in what they can do—and some of them are called superstars. A lot of players —it's said they don't know how; it's just that they're not looking for anybody."

If there was any problem with Barry's play last season, it was that he was too unselfish.

"Rick was playing the game the way it should be played," Golden State Coach Al Attles said. "It was textbook basketball. But we were off to a slow start, so I had to talk to him about being too unselfish. We were winning games when he scored more."

"Actually, I was planning to talk to Al about the same thing," Barry said. "I had gotten into a situation where I wasn't involved in the offense as much and hadn't been looking for shots as much. And I was getting ready to tell him it might help the team if I looked a little more. However, we had pretty good success last year when I was getting the ball to other people."

One benefit of Barry's looking to shoot more was that he was fouled more, and that was like money in the bank. The 6-foot-8 forward made 91.6 per cent of his foul shots to finish second to Buffalo's Ernie DiGregorio. He also set a record by hitting 60 straight.

The Warriors' defense suffered a notable decline last season, so a high-scoring offense was vital, and Barry was the key cog in that offense. In the regular season games in which Barry scored 30 or more points, the Warriors were 13-2. In games in which Barry scored less than 20, the Warriors were 13-20.

Guard Phil Smith, the Warriors' second leading

scorer with a 19-point average, was reportedly the target of much of Barry's ire for shooting too much.

But Barry and Attles each refuted that claim.

"There is no truth to the story that Phil and Rick don't get along," Attles said. "They have no problems. There is nothing in this business of Rick being jealous of Phil. Rick is not a petty person. This may have gotten started because they have such different styles. Rick goes his own way. Superstars always do. They all think differently. If Rick has a drawback—and it's not really a drawback—it's that he is not very patient. He can't understand why a guy can't play the game the way he does. That is a fault of all superstars. You may say of these people that they aren't regular guys. Well, they aren't."

Actually, the Warriors' biggest problem last season may have been the tremendous improvement of their Pacific Division rivals, the Portland Trail Blazers and the Lakers.

Barry had another outstanding season and Smith continued as one of the league's top offensive guards.

Forward Jamaal Wilkes, a slender 6-7 two-year veteran, averaged 17.7 points a game and was the team's second leading rebounder with 578, but he played out his option and signed with the Lakers.

Center Clifford Ray led the Warriors in rebounding with 615, but Golden State traded George Johnson, with whom Ray had shared the position.

The reason Johnson was deemed expendable was 7-foot rookie Robert Parish, who displayed promise of becoming the league's next great big man. Parish, who attended Centenary, had been mentioned as the probable No. 1 pick in the college draft, but his small-time college background apparently scared off several teams, and a half dozen players were selected before him.

However, North Carolina-Charlotte Coach Lee Rose had warned folks last year of what a great offensive player Parish was. Asked how his own underrated center, Cedric "Cornbread" Maxwell, had done against other top caliber players, Rose said, "Well, he did great in two games against Parish, held him to about 30 points both times."

"He can shoot and when you find that in a center you can wait for improvement in other departments," Attles said.

Parish averaged 9.1 points a game while sinking 50 per cent of his field goal attempts.

Guard Gus Williams, in his second year, averaged 9.3 points a game and the Warriors again had excellent reserves in Charles Dudley, Charles Johnson, Derrek Dickey and rookie Sonny Parker.

In the June draft, the Warriors selected Michigan's All-America guard Rickey Green and Louisville forward Wesley Cox as their first two choices.

Green's blazing speed and outstanding quickness make him a terror on defense and the fast break. He figured to go higher in the draft, but there was some apprehension about his outside shooting. He filed for hardship status after leading Michigan to the NCAA finals as a junior, but decided to polish his game with one more year of college ball. Cox also must prove he can shoot outside if he hopes to replace Wilkes at small forward.

PREDICTION: THIRD

Statistics for 1976-77 season

Player's name Years in NBA prior to 1976-77	G	M	FGM	FTM	PTS	AVG	FG%	REB	ASST
Barry, Rick (10 years)	79	2904	682	359	1723	21.8	.440	422	475
Davis, Dwight (10 years)	481	18,515	5024	2778	12,826	26.7	.450	3784	2326
Davis, Dwight (4 years)	33	552	55	49	159	4.8	.444	95	29
Dickey, Derrek (3 years)	307	7458	1075	627	2777	9.0	.422	1896	500
Dickey, Derrek (3 years)	49	856	158	45	361	7.4	.458	240	63
Dudley, Charles (3 years)	225	3996	609	179	1397	6.2	.478	1238	262
Dudley, Charles (3 years)	79	1682	220	129	569	7.2	.523	296	347
Johnson, Charles (4 years)	161	2311	294	241	829	5.1	.503	420	358
Johnson, Charles (4 years)	79	1196	255	49	559	7.1	.437	141	91
*McNeill, Larry (3 years)	289	5658	1101	206	2408	8.3	.431	820	575
*McNeill, Larry (3 years)	24	230	47	52	146	6.1	.420	75	6
Parish, Robert	216	3878	697	495	1889	8.7	.473	1153	169
Parish, Robert	77	1384	288	121	697	9.1	.503	543	74
Parker, Sonny	65	889	154	71	159	4.8	.527	173	59
Ray, Clifford (5 years)	77	2018	263	105	631	8.2	.584	615	112
Ray, Clifford (5 years)	399	11,216	1300	683	3283	8.2	.510	4289	1098
Rogers, Marshall	26	176	43	14	100	3.8	.371	11	10
Smith, Phil (2 years)	82	2880	631	295	1557	19.0	.479	332	328
Smith, Phil (2 years)	156	3848	880	450	2210	14.2	.476	516	497

Career statistics, not including those of the 1976-77 season

GOLDEN STATE WARRIORS

	G	M	FGM	FTM	PTS	AVG	FG%	REB	ASST
Williams, Gus	82	1930	325	112	762	9.3	.464	233	292
(1 year)	77	1728	365	106	903	11.7	.428	159	240

*—Combined N.Y. Nets-Golden State totals

Most Promising Rookies: Rickey Green, Wesley Cox. Green was acclaimed the fastest guard in the country and directed the Michigan powerhouse. An excellent ball-handler and an extremely dangerous defender because of his outstanding speed and quickness, Green was taken surprisingly low in the draft. The probable reason for this is Green's outside shooting is suspect. Cox, a 6-5 forward from Louisville, is sturdily built and has great leaping ability, but he too must prove his shooting ability to become an asset to the Warriors.

PERFORMANCE QUOTIENTS

Offense: The Warriors' offense was one of the best in the league and, if Parish continues to improve, could become awesome. Barry is one of the best offensive forwards in basketball history, an unerring shooter and an outstanding passer. He also is a better than 90 per cent shooter from the foul line. The Warriors will have a tough time replacing Jamaal Wilkes' scoring at the other forward spot. Smith, who had a 51-point game last season, is the Warriors' top scoring guard and could challenge for the scoring title if the Warriors did not have so many talented players. Smith averaged 19 points a game and his backcourt mate, Williams, averaged 9.3. On the bench, the Warriors had a 52 per cent shooter in guard Dudley. Reserve forward Parker also shot 52 per cent from the floor. Ray, the Warriors' starting center, rarely shoots, but when he did last season he connected 58 per cent of the time. Yet, Ray soon may be ousted from the starting lineup by Parish, who has the potential to become one of the NBA's top-scoring centers. **Perf. Qt.: 2.**

Defense: Ray is a good defensive center, but Parish still has a great deal to learn. Barry is one of the best defensive forwards in the league. Smith and Williams are average defenders, but reserve guard Johnson can be extremely tough defensively. **Perf. Qt.: 3.**

Rebounding: The combination of Ray and Parish gives the Warriors excellent rebounding from the center position. This is probably the weakest aspect of Barry's game. **Perf. Qt.: 3.**

Pacific Division

Seattle SuperSonics

Prediction: Fourth

Bill Russell tried to do it with long-distance humor. His cousin, Bob Hopkins, is going to try close-fisted mayhem.

The goal is the same, to lift the Seattle SuperSonics out of their perennial state of mediocrity and add the kind of excitement their nickname implies. The situation becomes just a little more critical this season since their neighbors in Portland are the NBA champions.

Although Hopkins is related to Russell, and worked for his cousin as assistant coach, he makes it clear he's his own man with his own methods. He also has the good sense to understand that he doesn't have the image of Russell, and he won't be allowed four years to build a winner.

"It's either me or them, and better me," Hopkins said in regard to survival. "There are several players that I don't think have shown they can play. I don't think they would be willing to sacrifice, to go through the work and training that will be necessary.

"I would rather not put myself on the spot to attempt to go through a season with those individuals."

Hopkins made clear the one quality he demands of his bigger players. "I'm looking for aggressiveness," he said. "I like guys who dish it out and who can take it. Guys 6-8 and 6-9 are paid to take punishment and hand it out, too. Our front line will be much more aggressive."

This was one of the chief criticisms leveled at the Sonics last season, and guard Slick Watts, known for his unabashed enthusiasm, said: "We don't have the killer instinct as a team. We can blame the coach, or management, but if we don't have the fight in our hearts, we can bring in Jesus Christ and it don't make no difference. We aren't physical enough. We don't fight enough."

Russell, at times, was an absentee coach and general manager although he was granted dictatorial powers to run the team by owner Sam Schulman. Some of his players complained they didn't know what was expected of them, and even the adoring fans in Seattle grew weary of the wise-cracking Russell. At one game in March, while the Sonics were absorbing a 105-85 rout by Cleveland, thousands of fans jeered them and one yelled out, "Hey Schulman, put somebody in for Russell."

After Seattle failed to qualify for the playoffs, although he still had a year remaining on his $250,000 a year contract, Russell said, "I have reached a point in my career where I want to pursue other activities."

Hopkins, who played six years in the NBA with the old Syracuse Nationals, became frustrated himself at times when Russell failed to get more closely involved with his players, and he has an inclination to teach.

The 42-year-old Hopkins promised a housecleaning when he took over, and his first big move was to trade 7-2 center Tom Burleson and guard Bob Wilkerson to Denver for center Marvin Webster and veteran forwards Paul Silas and Willie Wise.

It is ironic—and perhaps preordained—that Burleson would be the first to go, since he had been the pet project of Russell but failed in three years to live up to his potential.

"We got three players I really wanted," said Hopkins. "Silas is very physical, one of the premier rebounders in the league, and he still has good speed. Wise is physical, too, and he's a great outside shooter."

The key acquisition, of course, was Webster, another young giant who experienced more difficulty than expected in his first two years in the pros. However, part of the problem was caused by a kidney ailment that forced him to miss most of his rookie campaign.

Nicknamed "The Human Eraser" at Morgan State because of his shot-blocking and defensive work, the 7-1 Webster reassured Seattle fans as to the merits of the deal.

"No doubt about it, Seattle got the best of that trade," he said. "I'm a good ballplayer and I can start for anybody. But I don't want anybody to think I'm a savior or a franchise or anything like that. Maybe I could be, but I don't want anybody to think that right off."

If modesty caught up with Webster, it didn't prevent Silas from adding his own opinion. "Marvin is an up-and-coming center," he said. "I think he could some day be in the class of a Jabbar or a Walton. He's the type of player you can build a team around."

The additions of Wise and Silas are expected to give the Sonics short-term help. Lenny Wilkens, the new director of player personnel, said, "This definitely gives us a front line that can start right away. Our biggest problem last year was the lack of any type of consistency in our front line play. We feel we can now be consistent and competitive and we won't be intimidated."

Hopkins would like to have a running team because that "can cover up a lot of mistakes." A prerequisite for this, however, is strong rebounding, a virtue Seattle never seems to have. Hopkins feels he has solved this problem to a degree with the acquisitions of Webster and 6-11 Jack Sikma, the Sonics' first round draft choice. Sikma averaged 27 points and 15 rebounds a game at Illinois Wesleyan last season.

"In the first round we weren't going for the best athlete," Hopkins said. "We needed a center, and we wanted one who can shoot away from the basket and pull away the Waltons and the Jabbars. Sikma can hit those 15- and 18-footers. He's an outstanding rebounder. He's intimidating, but not a great shot blocker. He's intelligent, doesn't force many bad shots, he draws fouls and he has good speed. He's a Dan Issel type."

The Sonics are expecting to get double figure rebounding from Webster, and another strong man off the boards is 6-10 Mike Green, who can be used at center or power forward. Green had 503 rebounds last season, second on the team behind Burleson's 551.

The brunt of the Seattle scoring last season was concentrated in the backcourt. Fred Brown led the team with a 17.2 average and Watts was next at 13.0. However, there was strong speculation that Hopkins was looking to trade Brown, and Watts, who had a contract disagreement last season, also is a candidate to move on although he is a very popular figure in Seattle.

"We never got involved in a fight all last season," Hopkins complained. "But when people try to intimidate you and it comes down to you or them, there's gonna be a fight."

When he said it, he wasn't joking.

PREDICTION: FOURTH

Statistics for 1976-77 season

Career statistics, not including those of the 1976-77 season

Player's name Years in NBA prior to 1976-77	G	M	FGM	FTM	PTS	AVG	FG%	REB	ASST
Brown, Fred (5 years)	72	2098	534	168	1236	17.2	.479	232	176
Green, Mike (5 years)	351	10,365	2587	837	6011	17.1	.470	1416	1403
Green, Mike	76	1928	290	166	746	9.8	.441	503	120
†(3 years)	214	5924	1345	548	3239	15.1	.495	1852	247
Johnson, Dennis	81	1667	285	179	749	9.2	.504	302	123
*Love, Bob	59	1174	162	109	433	7.3	.379	198	48
(10 years)	730	23,946	5285	2892	13,462	18.4	.431	4455	1075
Norwood, Willie	76	1647	216	151	583	7.7	.469	292	99
(5 years)	319	5083	928	572	2428	7.6	.501	1186	232
Oleynick, Frank	50	516	81	39	201	4.0	.363	45	60
(1 year)	52	650	127	53	307	5.9	.402	45	53
Seals, Bruce	81	1977	378	138	894	11.0	.444	354	93
(1 year)	81	2435	388	181	957	11.8	.436	507	119
**Silas, Paul	81	1959	206	170	582	7.2	.360	606	132
(12 years)	927	27,306	3620	2712	9952	10.7	.441	10,074	2114
Tolson, Dean	60	587	137	85	359	6.0	.566	157	27
(1 year)	19	87	16	11	43	2.3	.432	22	5
Watts, Slick	79	2627	428	172	1028	13.0	.422	307	630
(3 years)	226	6256	863	392	2118	9.4	.416	809	1511
***Weatherspoon, Nick	62	1657	310	91	711	11.5	.449	428	53
(3 years)	211	3646	673	295	1641	7.8	.448	1017	144
**Webster, Marvin	80	1276	198	143	539	6.7	.495	484	62
†(1 year)	38	398	55	55	165	4.3	.462	174	30

SEATTLE SUPERSONICS

	G	M	FGM	FTM	PTS	AVG	FG%	REB	ASST
**Wise, Willie	75	1403	237	142	616	8.2	.462	253	142
†(7 years)	475	17,025	3478	2133	9110	19.2	.480	4322	1452

*—Combined Nets-Seattle totals
**—Acquired from Denver
***—Combined Washington-Seattle totals
†—ABA totals

Most Promising Rookies: Jack Sikma, Joe Hassett. Rebounding strength was the first order of business for new Coach Bob Hopkins, and after trading for Marvin Webster he used his first-round pick to choose Sikma, a 6-11 center from Illinois Wesleyan. Sikma averaged 27 points and 15.4 rebounds last season. Hassett, selected in the third round, is a 6-5 guard who averaged 19 points in his senior year at Providence.

PERFORMANCE QUOTIENTS

Offense: It was obvious the Sonics had to inject better balance into their attack, and new Coach Bob Hopkins hopes he has accomplished this with the addition of a new front line—veteran forwards Silas and Wise and centers Webster and Jack Sikma, a rookie. Seattle had one of the poorer offenses in the NBA last season, averaging 104 points a game and a below-average 45 per cent accuracy rating, and the problem was a serious lack of frontcourt help. The backcourt duo of Brown and Watts led the scoring list with averages of 17.2 and 13.0, respectively, and the only big men to hit double figures were Weatherspoon (11.5) and Seals (11.0). Wise, an excellent outside shooter, compiled a 19.2 average in seven years in the ABA, although he tailed off to 8.2 as a part-timer at Denver last season. Silas is coming off a poor campaign with the Nuggets; he averaged 7.2 points, shooting only 36 per cent. **Perf. Qt.: 5.**

Defense: There was a slight improvement on defense last season as the Sonics yielded 105.5 points, and it is felt that Webster will be even more effective than Tom Burleson who was in clogging up the middle. Green can be intimidating close to the basket and he registered a team-high 129 blocked shots. Watts, after leading the league in 1975-76 with 261 steals and being named to the All-Defensive team, picked off only 214 last season. **Perf. Qt.: 3.**

Rebounding: This was another relatively weak department, Burleson taking team honors with only 551. Webster, in about two-thirds of Burleson's playing time, snatched 484 at Denver, and should be able to do better if used on a regular basis. Sikma is an excellent rebounder and Silas, credited with 606 rebounds last season, long has been one of the better rebounding forwards in the game. **Perf. Qt.: 3.**

Pacific Division

Phoenix Suns

Prediction: Fifth

The Phoenix Suns, the Cinderella team of the 1976 playoffs, played the role out during the 1976-77 season by turning into a pumpkin.

Alvan Adams, the 1976 Rookie of the Year, missed 10 games with an ankle injury and then was slow getting into shape. Forwards Gar Heard and Curtis Perry lasted only a half-season each before being sidelined with injuries. Then, there were numerous minor injuries to other players and the net result was a 34-48 record and a last-place finish in the Pacific Division.

The injuries to Heard and Perry, the Suns' muscle men, turned Phoenix into the worst rebounding team in the NBA.

The Suns' front line problems placed even more of an offensive burden on guard Paul Westphal, and he responded by making the NBA All-Star team, and leading the West to victory. He also led the Suns in scoring with a 21.3 average and in assists with 459.

Westphal saved the All-Star victory with a key defensive play. Ironically, that was the one aspect of his game that the Suns were worried about when they dealt high-scoring Charlie Scott to the Celtics for him. "He has made great strides defensively, and that has been our concern," said General Manager Jerry Colangelo.

Ricky Sobers, after an excellent rookie season, averaged 13.6 points a game, but lost his starting job to rookie Ron Lee, who averaged 10.2 points and played tough defense.

"And what can you say about Ronnie Lee?" Phoenix Coach John MacLeod said. "He's intense, enthusiastic and he's just going to get better."

Lee and fellow rookie Ira Terrell, a forward, were the only two Suns players to go through the season without an injury and play all 82 games.

"Ira Terrell got over 1700 minutes of playing time, mostly as a starter, and proved he's capable of becoming a good NBA player," MacLeod said.

But MacLeod had to settle for esthetic victories last season, such as: "Considering the high expectations everyone had for this year, it was a tribute to the type of young men we have playing for the Suns that the club morale remained so high."

But MacLeod has good reason to be optimistic about this season as long as Perry recovers from his back problems and Heard from his stress fracture. While there are no anxieties about Heard's recovery, Perry's status has the Suns worried.

The Suns' team physician, Dr. Paul Steingard, said, "Curtis has a complicated back problem, but we certainly expect him to play again next year. The toughest thing to prescribe in medicine is rest and that's exactly the prescription for Curtis at this time."

Explaining his ailment, Perry said, "What I've got is a fracture at a point on a vertebrae, and fractures heal.

"I'm not supposed to do anything but lay around," he said during the spring. "It's boring, but I'm healing.

There's still a little pain in the back, but nothing compared with what I had."

If everything works as MacLeod hopes, though, either Perry or Heard will be forced to the bench. The Suns' master plan calls for rookie Bayard Forrest to take over the center position with Adams moving to forward. This would give Phoenix more scoring punch, since Perry and Heard are primarily rebounders.

Forrest, 6-10, led little-known Grand Canyon College of Phoenix to the NAIA championship in 1975. The three-time NAIA All-America was drafted in the second round of the 1976 draft by the Seattle SuperSonics, but decided instead to play for the Fellowship of Christian Athletes' barnstorming group, Athletes in Action.

AIA pulled off a number of upsets against its collegiate competition, the most notable a victory over the University of San Francisco, which was ranked No. 1 and undefeated at the time. Forrest was Athletes In Action's leading rebounder and No. 2 scorer.

When it became obvious he still was hesitant about signing with the Sonics, they traded the rights to him to the Suns for a second-round pick in the 1979 draft and an undisclosed amount of money.

Forrest was a great deal more eager to join the Suns and, at the announcement of his signing, said, "This is something I've looked forward to ever since the day I enrolled at Grand Canyon College."

The year with AIA increased Forrest's market value. As Jerry Colangelo explained, "A year with Athletes In Action was like getting a year in major college competition for Bayard. It made him a much better player in every respect and he would have been a cinch firstrounder this time."

Forrest, like Adams, is slightly built for an NBA

center, but the Suns planned to build him up a bit during the summer. Adams has relied on his quickness during his two-year career and established himself as one of the league's best-passing centers. He had 450 assists as a rookie and 322 last season.

But Colangelo said, "Forrest is an even better passer than Adams."

Asked his reaction to the proposed shift to forward, Adams said, "I had pretty good success at center. But, on the other hand, you don't get banged around as much at forward. I wasn't as big as any of the other centers in the league and I'm actually not as big as many of the forwards. I guess what I am is a real big guard."

The Suns' top draft pick was Walter Davis, a slender 6-6 forward with great jumping ability and the speed and shot to play in the backcourt. He may get playing time in both places, as the Van Arsdale twins, guard Dick and swingman Tom, both have retired.

"I played guard on the Olympic team and I have played both forward and guard at North Carolina," Davis said. "I'm confident and comfortable at each position and I don't really care where I play. I just want to contribute as much to the team as I can."

Westphal and Adams, who had an 18-point scoring average, again will lead the Suns. But whether or not Phoenix makes it back to the playoffs may depend on the two newcomers, Forrest and Davis.

PREDICTION: FIFTH

Statistics for 1976-77 season

Career statistics, not including those of the 1976-77 season

Player's name / Years in NBA prior to 1976-77	G	M	FGM	FTM	PTS	AVG	FG%	REB	ASST
Adams, Alvan (1 year)	72	2278	522	252	1296	18.0	.474	652	322
Awtrey, Dennis (6 years)	80	2656	629	261	1519	19.0	.469	727	450
	72	1760	160	91	411	5.7	.429	356	182
Erickson, Keith (11 years)	434	8742	2097	500	2480	5.7	.472	2296	951
	50	949	142	37	321	6.4	.483	144	104
Feher, Butch	716	17,892	2872	1186	6930	9.7	.433	3304	1887
	48	487	86	76	248	5.2	.531	74	36
Heard, Garfield (6 years)	46	1363	173	100	446	9.7	.379	440	89
Lee, Ron	438	11,862	1926	732	4584	10.5	.417	3705	720
	82	1849	347	142	836	10.2	.441	299	263
Perry, Curtis (6 years)	44	1391	179	112	470	10.7	.432	395	79
Schlueter, Dale (8 years)	391	11,447	1615	607	3837	9.8	.457	3594	779
	39	337	26	18	70	1.8	.361	80	38
Sobers, Ricky (1 year)	537	9178	1142	751	3035	5.7	.502	2933	864
Terrell, Ira	79	2005	414	243	1071	13.6	.496	234	238
	78	1898	280	158	718	9.2	.449	259	215
	78	1751	277	111	665	8.5	.508	387	103
Westphal, Paul (4 years)	81	2600	682	362	1726	21.3	.518	190	459
	306	6188	268	663	3315	10.8	.494	632	915

Most Promising Rookies: Walter Davis, Billy McKinney. Davis, a 6-6 forward from North Carolina, is an unselfish player capable of contributing to the Suns in a number of ways. An extremely consistent and team-oriented player, Davis averaged 14.3 points as a freshman, 16.1 as a sophomore, 16.6 as a junior and 15.5 as a senior. His career field goal percentage was .531 and he also is an outstanding leaper. Finally, he was one of North Carolina's clutch performers, well able to withstand any pressure. Davis proved his versatility in the Olympics by switching to guard. McKinney, who is not quite 6-feet tall, averaged 20.6 points a game for Northwestern with his excellent outside shooting.

PERFORMANCE QUOTIENTS

Offense: Westphal has developed into one of the top guards in the NBA and was selected to last season's NBA All-Star team. Westphal averaged 21.3 points a game for the Suns and his shooting percentage was a remarkable .518. At the same time, Westphal set up teammates often enough to rank ninth in the league in assists with an average of 5.7 a game. Last season the Suns ran into much stiffer competition in the Pacific Division and a rash of injuries. The combination of the two proved deadly, but the Suns continued to perform as a disciplined unit as evidenced by the fact they were fourth in the league in assists, although 15th in scoring. Adams recuperated from an early-season injury to average 18 points a game and total 322 assists. Sobers had an exceptionally good shooting percentage of .496 in compiling a 13.6 scoring average and rookie guard Lee also shot better than expected, 44.1 per cent, to average 10.2. Erickson missed more than 30 games last season, which cost the Suns a valuable offensive lift off the bench. His return to health, along with Heard and Perry, will help, as will the addition of Davis. **Perf. Qt.: 3.**

Defense: Sobers and Lee give the Suns the best defensive backcourt in the league. Both play excellent defense, but Lee positively brutalizes opponents. However, Lee and Sobers usually are not on the court at the same time as each is used to complement Westphal in the backcourt. The Suns had the fifth best defense in the league last year and should maintain that lofty status. **Perf. Qt.: 2.**

Rebounding: This is why the Suns fell from championship runnerup to also-ran last season. The Suns were the worst rebounding team in the league after Heard and Perry were injured. Their return and the addition of Bayard Forrest should improve things some. The slender 6-10 Forrest will have to do a top job under the boards for the Suns to regain a spot in the playoffs. **Perf. Qt.: 4.**

Super Features, Action Profiles

Exciting, exclusive stories about pro basketball, plus behind the scenes visits with such stars as Julius Erving, Bill Walton, Kareem Abdul-Jabbar, Dave Cowens, Moses Malone, Bobby Jones and Bob McAdoo

If at First . . .

It certainly did not have the air of being a momentous night for the New York Nets.

As General Manager Bill Melchionni described it: "We were just kicking around names."

Bubbles Hawkins was one of those names being kicked around. All the names had been kicked not only around, but out of the National Basketball Association.

Hawkins had had his chance, such as it was, with the Golden State Warriors and was found lacking.

There are dozens of players each season whose careers are laid to rest in the "almost" category. But, every once in a while, one of these players resurrects his basketball career from the ashes.

The Philadelphia 76ers' Steve Mix did, as did the New Orleans Jazz' Otto Moore and the Chicago Bulls' Wilbur Holland.

But none achieved the feat in as spectacular a fashion as Hawkins, a 6-4 guard with a tremendously long reach.

One of the fellows Melchionni had been kicking around names with was Duke's assistant athletic director Jeff Mullins, who had seen Bubbles in action for the Warriors.

Never having seen Hawkins, Melchionni sought a second opinion. He called the Warriors' Rick Barry.

"Rick's usually pretty critical," Melchionni said, "and he said the guy could play a little bit. That's a pretty strong recommendation from Rick because he usually doesn't say anyone can play except himself."

Hawkins was about to embark on his new career as a summons server in his native Detroit when Melchionni called and asked him to join the Nets. The Nets were on the road when Hawkins arrived at New York, so Melchionni, who retired two years ago, worked out with his latest acquisition.

Afterwards, according to Melchionni, "I knew he had some talent."

It was talent Hawkins had not given up hope of using when he was cut the day before the season began.

"I was hoping to get picked up by someone, but I wasn't confident," Hawkins said. "I was anticipating being out of the game a year, but I was intent on coming back and playing. I was hoping by February I would be able to get in contact with a few teams."

Among the teams Hawkins had tried to interest were the Denver Nuggets, the Los Angeles Lakers and the Buffalo Braves.

If a person ever found himself in the right place at the right time, though, it was Hawkins. Shortly after Bubbles joined the Nets, the team's top-scoring guard, Nate Archibald, was injured—he was to miss the rest of the season. Then, as Hawkins began to get increased playing time, the Nets traded guard John Williamson to the Indiana Pacers, at the same time releasing forward Rich Jones. It was a small but disgusted group of fans on hand for the Nets' first game after the completion of the massive housecleaning.

But Hawkins scored 18 points in the final 16 minutes

to lead the Nets past the Boston Celtics. Then he scored 24 points as the Nets upset the 76ers in Philadelphia and 37 in leading the Nets to victory over the Cavaliers in Cleveland. By the end of New York's remarkable three-game winning streak, Nets fans had a new hero.

"I just try to beat my man and make something happen," said Hawkins, who not only made things happen, but did it with a flair. Although he was tried briefly as a starter, Hawkins preferred coming off the bench. And, whenever the Nets were still in contention in the closing minutes, Hawkins almost certainly was going to take the big shots.

"I don't mind shooting down the stretch. I just like to have my presence felt," said Hawkins, who averaged 19.3 points a game for the Nets. "If there's no pressure, it's no fun."

"He's got something—who knows what you should call it—charisma, I guess," Nets Coach Kevin Loughery said. "The Doc [Julius Erving] had unbelievable charisma because he was so great. But here is a kid who is out of the league, comes back and scores a point a minute some nights. I guess our fans were ready for a new name, for a guy with a fresh face who smiles the way he does out there. All I know is that Bubbles Hawkins has become a hero just when we needed one."

The Bulls did not need a hero, but certainly were looking for a shooting guard when they signed Holland. The 6-foot guard had been cut by the Atlanta Hawks.

Gene Tormohlen, who had drafted Holland for the Hawks, since had moved to the Bulls as an assistant coach and Holland called to ask for a tryout after being cut.

"If he can't play, I'll pay his salary," Tormohlen told Chicago Coach Ed Badger.

Holland saved Tormohlen's money by moving into the starting lineup within a month and averaging 14.9 points a game with a shooting percentage of .454, mostly on long-range bombs.

The dean of the free agent refugees, though, is the 76ers' Mix. The 6-foot-7 forward lost his starting position to Erving, but Mix said, "I think I had my best year shooting and defensively."

Mix, who has been cut by more teams than he would care to admit, averaged 10.5 points and 5.1 rebounds in his role as a reserve.

The previous season, as a starter, Mix had averaged 13.9 points and 8.6 rebounds. Still, Mix does not believe his best years are behind him.

"I can play another three or four years," he said. "My game's not predicated on speed or jumping like some players. I think a guy like me can stay around longer than some players whose biggest assets are running and jumping."

Moore, whose career appeared ended three years ago before he was given one last chance by the Jazz, played more than 2000 minutes and was New Orleans' leading rebounder with 636 and top shot blocker with 117.

Rivalry with Respect

A few years ago, nowhere in sports was there a more heated rivalry than the one between Bill Russell and Wilt Chamberlain. So intense were their feelings, so strong their emotions, these giants among men carried on a feud off the court that gained as much attention as the elbows they dug into each other under the baskets.

That was the kind of rivalry a fan could lick his chops over. Russell and Chamberlain, the two most dominant figures of their time, kicking and clawing at each other during a game, then sniping at and baiting each other in public.

It wasn't their way to utter empty phrases pretending respect for each other. Not even in retirement did either relent; once, when Russell was hosting a radio talk show in Los Angeles, he was asked by a caller why he didn't invite Chamberlain to appear as a guest.

"Well," Russell answered, "it's pretty hard to interview someone you don't talk to."

Chamberlain struck at Russell in his autobiography, writing, "He actually seemed to think the Celtics' playoff wins over my teams made him a better man than me—a better human being—and that gave him the right to sit in judgment on me, like some omniscient God."

Chamberlain then added, "It may sound like sour grapes, but I really think Bill is a shallower man for all his basketball triumphs, and rather than my being angry or envious over his victories and his gloating and his raps at me, I feel sorry for him."

This piece of the past was reproduced here to remind fans of what not to expect in the present. For while another great rivalry has come along to match the grip Chamberlain and Russell once held on the public's imagination, the present combatants have no desire whatsoever to sound off once the game is over.

But when it comes to playing basketball, Kareem Abdul-Jabbar of the Los Angeles Lakers and Bill Walton of the Portland Trail Blazers are worthy successors to Russell and Chamberlain as an awesome rivalry. It took Walton two years to shake off a string of injuries and clear his head, but last season he finally showed his credentials as the most gifted all-around player in the game.

Abdul-Jabbar, of course, long before had proved himself the most dominant figure in basketball.

Both men had played at UCLA, Abdul-Jabbar graduating a year before Walton started, and together they accounted for five of the record 10 NCAA championships John Wooden won for the school. The first professional meeting between these two titans was anticipated with great expectations, but it was an embarrassing bomb. On Jan. 19, 1975, at Milwaukee, Abdul-Jabbar scored 50 points, grabbed 15 rebounds and had 11 assists to lead the Bucks, his old team, to a 122-108 victory over Portland. Walton had seven points, six rebounds and seven assists.

Walton summed up the experience by saying, "It was fun playing against him."

It took two years, though, before Walton proved it could be fun. And last season it was, for him and for fans all across the country who enjoy a super rivalry. It was climaxed in the playoff semifinals, when Abdul-Jabbar squared off against Walton in a head-to-head duel that reached heights all other mortals had to look up to.

That playoff series only added further fuel to what is bound to be a raging controversy for the next few years—which of the two is better. Abdul-Jabbar had the better figures for four games, outscoring Walton 121-77, outrebounding him 64-59, and blocking more shots, 15-9. But Walton was the driving force as Portland swept the series and then went on to shock Philadelphia for the championship.

"Comparisons are inevitable," Abdul-Jabbar said once his season was ended. "We both play the same position and we both have a lot of skill. But I look at Walton as someone who plays for a team. It's the team I worry about, not the individual player. I know what he can do, and he knows what I can do, but 95 per cent of the time that our teams meet, neither of us really has anything to do with the actual outcome."

Walton, known to be outspoken on controversial subjects, also tends to play down the rivalry. "It's no big deal," he said before the series began, all the while admitting he was excited at the prospect of the encounter. "As Kareem gets older he gets smarter. Physically he's in his prime. I think he's playing the best of his life."

This, incidentally, is a theory wholly supported by Abdul-Jabbar, who at 30 is six years older than Walton. The 7-2 center led the Lakers to a 53-29 regular season record, the best in the NBA, for which he was selected the Most Valuable Player for the fifth time in the last seven years. Russell is the only other player to win the MVP five times.

When he was told of his honor, Abdul-Jabbar said, "I don't think I can play any better or with any more consistency. Once a player reaches his late twenties or early thirties his physical ability and knowledge of the game begin to mesh. That's when a player is at his peak.

"Since I've been in Los Angeles [two years], I believe I've been getting the most out of my potential. I've matured as a player and that's the most important part of anybody's development."

Walton, who was a distant runnerup to Abdul-Jabbar in the MVP voting, is a different kind of player. At 6-11, he is three inches shorter than Abdul-Jabbar, and the Blazers aren't as reliant on him rolling up points. The intense redhead is the team captain and leader, a playmaker with extraordinary court awareness. He directs the offense, is intimidating on defense, and in many ways serves as an on-court coach.

In the third game of the series against Los Angeles, the Blazers were trailing, 81-77, on their home court with a little more than nine minutes to play. In the space of six minutes, Walton scored 14 of his team's 16 points to give Portland a 93-84 lead and, for all practicality, the series.

"What can you say," Portland Coach Jack Ramsay asked when he was questioned about Walton after that performance. "He does whatever is necessary to win. Always. This time we needed his scoring, so he scored. But if it's defense, or rebounding, or passing, whatever it is, he does it. His game has no flaw. And his determination is unbelievable. When he gets that look on his face, you just know he can do anything that has to be done."

Kareem Abdul-Jabbar vs. Bill Walton? They really can't be compared by the same measuring stick. During the regular season, Abdul-Jabbar averaged 26.2 per game to Walton's 18.6, but Walton led the NBA in rebounding (14.4 average) and blocked shots (3.25), with Abdul-Jabbar second in both departments.

Walton sat out 17 games with three different injuries, and Portland lost 12 of them. With Walton in the lineup, the Trail Blazers had a 44-21 record for a .667 percentage, better than any other team compiled. The Lakers' percentage was .646.

In his previous two years in the NBA, Walton suffered nine broken bones and twice underwent surgery, limiting him to 86 games. In the eight years Abdul-Jabbar has been a pro, only twice has he played in less than 81 games, and this has to be an important factor in comparing the two.

"If Kareem has a drawback it's that I don't think he's a dominant leader," said Washington Coach Dick Motta. "He doesn't play with quite the charisma Walton does, but over the long run I'd take him over Walton. You can depend on him. He doesn't get hurt and he's going to come through for you in the big games."

The Lakers won three of four regular season games from Portland with Abdul-Jabbar getting the better of Walton, at least statistically. Los Angeles won the first game, 99-96, with Kareem getting 32 points to Walton's 26, and the second in overtime, 115-111, Abdul-Jabbar scoring 35 and Walton 28. Walton didn't play in the third meeting and Abdul-Jabbar led Los Angeles to a 104-99 triumph with 25 points.

When the teams met for the fourth time, the Lakers already had clinched the Pacific Division championship and with Abdul-Jabbar playing only 23 minutes, they were wiped out, 145-116. Walton scored 19 points to eight for Kareem.

It is worth pointing out that when they won those three games, the Lakers had the services of forward Kermit Washington, a strong rebounder who helped neutralize Portland's powerful Maurice Lucas. But Washington suffered a knee injury February 11 and wasn't available for the playoffs.

Be that as it may, the big attraction of the playoff series was Abdul-Jabbar against Walton, and it was the younger man who won the duel since it was his team that swept into the finals.

"Walton believes in his talent," Abdul-Jabbar said graciously of his rival. "He tests his skill rather than using muscle to hang on me. It's a challenge to play against a guy this good, on a level above what I go through most nights. It's not so much even winning. It's expressing yourself."

Who is the better player?

"Kareem is the best player in basketball," says his coach, Jerry West. "He's the most awesome force in the NBA. Sometimes I feel sorry for him out there since we don't help him enough. Bill Walton is a magnificent basketball player, but he's the second best center in basketball."

On the other side of the court, after Walton led Portland to its sweep over the Lakers, Maurice Lucas asked facetiously "If Kareem is the best, what does that make Bill?"

From here on out, the most exciting rivalry in basketball can only get hotter.

The Doctor Was Out

As delightful a contraption as the television set is, you wonder what worldly good it would have done anyone 100 years ago when there weren't any shows to watch. The same with an automobile in the hands of a caveman, without a gas station in sight.

The point is, you can have the most marvelous, most miraculous, most modernistic gadget at your fingertips, but you may as well be back in the cave if you don't know how to use it.

Such a sorry situation seemed to exist last season in Philadelphia, where there was the most talented doctor of his kind in the house, but they forgot to let him operate. It was almost as if the New York Yankees of 55 years ago had decided to allow Babe Ruth to remain a pitcher.

There is an ironic twist to Julius Erving's introduction to Philadelphia. The 76ers wanted the world's most spectacular basketball player to blend his unique talents into a team concept. Certainly, this is an admirable goal. But with all their incredible individual ability, the 76ers never did achieve this unity and they crashed in the championship finals against a Portland team that played as an extension of one another.

The 76ers, seemingly in desperation, began looking for Erving, and he averaged 30.3 points a game in the series. But that wasn't enough to offset George McGinnis' slump and the Blazers' teamwork.

In the regular season, it wasn't simply a matter of Erving falling more than seven points shy of his per-game average for five previous years in the pros, but he was inhibited in his accustomed role as a free-floating magician with the kind of moves that have never before been seen.

Kevin Loughery, who had coached Erving to two ABA championships with the New York Nets, was bewildered the first time his club played the 76ers last season and commented that Dr. J. "was like a foreigner in another country."

"Maybe it's because he didn't get the ball as much as he did here," Loughery said. "I don't think he's happy playing basketball. He may be happy in life but not on the court. I don't think he likes the role he's playing.

"Julius is simply the most exciting player I've ever seen and he's a winner. I don't think he should be put in that position for basketball's sake. It's a shame for the people to miss the greatest show in basketball."

Erving, who went to Philadelphia last fall in a $6-million deal after failing to reach a contract settlement with the Nets, agreed in part with his former coach, freely admitting, "I'm not the same player I was last year. I'm not doing things as spectacularly this year. I don't take as many shots and I don't do as many things."

Teammate McGinnis perhaps put it best when he said, "You're never going to see Dr. J. again, that's over, but Julius Erving is a pretty good basketball player too."

Erving, as great as he is, wasn't accepted by his new teammates for the first half of the season, although toward the end of the campaign he started to take more control. He certainly earned the respect of those he played with.

"He's one of the greatest basketball players your eyes will ever witness," Coach Gene Shue said. "It's absolutely refreshing to know someone like Doc. He came to our team in a difficult situation . . . his whole attitude was to blend in with the team, to do whatever he had to do. In addition to being a fine basketball player and a leader, he has a great attitude toward life and he's a gentleman."

Dr. J. was one of only two 76ers to play in all 82 games (Caldwell Jones was the other), and he led the team in minutes played (2940) and scoring average (21.6), and was second in assists (306), rebounds (695), steals (159) and blocked shots (113).

Erving's contract with Philadelphia calls for him to receive some $3-million, and while it is highly debatable whether any athlete is worth that kind of money, there is no question that the Doctor returned some dividends. On his first swing through the league, record crowds turned out virtually everywhere to witness the magic they had only heard of before.

In Atlanta, for example, Erving attracted a crowd of more than 15,000. The next night, when the Hawks played Kansas City, the attendance was a lonesome 1067. When the Doctor paid a house call to the New Orleans Superdome, an NBA record crowd of more than 27,000 turned out.

"There's been great pressure on him throughout the country," said Philadelphia General Manager Pat Williams. "Every place we go it's like a three-ring circus.

He has had an impact in Philadelphia which is unequalled."

Added McGinnis, "People expect so much of him. I'd hate to have that kind of pressure on me. Every time he puts his hand on a basketball he disappoints people if he doesn't do something that hasn't been done before."

With his myriad moves on the court, you'd think Erving would have nothing left for life. But the 6-7, 27-year-old New York native is full of surprises even when he talks. For example, assessing all the advantages he has enjoyed, he commented, "I have been given the opportunity to be a famous person, a rich person, someone who can command attention when he speaks. I have a chance to turn these dreams into things more positive, constructive, progressive . . . doing God's work, promoting family unity and good will.

"Let's have more people in the world look for the good in people. All people have some good in them."

As serious as he is about using his position to help others, one can't help thinking how much happier basketball fans would be if the old Doctor made a comeback.

It brings to mind, wishfully, an offhand remark Erving made midway through last season, "I'm seriously thinking of bringing Dr. J. out of the closet."

NBA WEST: MVPs and All-Stars

Norm Van Lier
Chicago Bulls

NBA WEST: MVPs

Bobby Jones
Denver Nuggets

Bob Lanier
Detroit Pistons

NBA WEST: MVPs

Rick Barry
Golden State Warriors

Billy Knight
Indiana Pacers

NBA WEST: MVPs

Ron Boone
Kansas City Kings

Kareem Abdul-Jabbar
Los Angeles Lakers

NBA WEST: MVPs

Brian Winters
Milwaukee Bucks

Alvan Adams
Phoenix Suns

NBA WEST: MVPs

Bill Walton
Portland Trail Blazers

Fred Brown
Seattle SuperSonics

NBA WEST: All-Stars

Rick Barry
Forward
Golden State Warriors

David Thompson
Forward
Denver Nuggets

NBA WEST: All-Stars

Kareem Abdul-Jabbar
Center
Los Angeles Lakers

Ron Boone
Guard
Kansas City Kings

NBA WEST: All-Stars

Norm Van Lier
Guard
Chicago Bulls

The Cream of the Crop

They said Adrian Dantley was too small to make it as a forward in the National Basketball Association, just as they had said David Thompson was too small for the pro wars under the backboard.

Dantley, only 6-foot-5, had been a college All-America at Notre Dame by using his body, a chunk of granite, to muscle his way by and through his opponents. But, obviously, he would not be able to do the same to the monsters roaming through the NBA.

Naive rookie that he was, Dantley never realized this fact and averaged 20.3 points a game in his first season with the Buffalo Braves, despite drawing double coverage from many teams. His outstanding performance made him a runaway choice as the NBA's Rookie of the Year in a season when many talented newcomers made their presence felt.

Although Dantley was the top college freshman during the 1973-74 season and a first-team All-America the next two seasons before making himself eligible for the NBA draft as a hardship case, Dantley was only the sixth player chosen.

"I know I would have been the first player picked if

I was 6-7," Dantley said. "They were looking at the inches rather than the player."

Dantley never has looked like the ideal forward; he only has played like it.

Dantley was a 6-2 freshman at DeMatha High School in Hyattsville, Md., when he first began to attract attention. Despite being a pudgy 231-pounder, Dantley quickly gained recognition as one of the best players ever in the basketball-rich Washington, D.C., area. The recruiters fought a spirited battle for Dantley and Notre Dame's Digger Phelps was the winner.

His spectacular collegiate career had an Olympic postscript as Dantley led the United States to the gold medal in Montreal. He averaged 20 points a game during the Olympics and scored 30 points in the championship game against Yugoslavia.

"I never worked harder for anything in my life than the Olympics," he said.

But that may not be true; Dantley's freshman year at Notre Dame was an academic nightmare, although it never showed in his play. The transition to college was an extremely difficult one for Dantley and Phelps several times had to chase his young star away from practice and insist he spend the time studying instead. An indication of his perseverance is the fact Dantley so applied himself to his studies he would have graduated after three years if it had not been for his Olympic participation. His natural talents are incredible, but Dantley has worked doggedly throughout his career to fulfill his potential.

"People were saying that I wasn't a player," said Dantley, whose dieting during his freshman year caused him to collapse in a game. "That I was too fat, too slow, too short, that I got easy points at Notre Dame."

That was the type of thinking which caused five

teams to pass over Dantley before the Braves chose him. Despite his bulk, Dantley has an exceptionally quick first step, an asset often overlooked because of the way he muscles his way to the basket. Although they may have been cool to Dantley before his arrival in the pros, NBA coaches were quickly impressed.

"His best skill is in his reaction to defensive pressure," said Joe Mullaney, who took over as Braves' coach in mid-season.

"I don't understand why he wasn't the No. 1 pick in the draft," said Los Angeles Coach Jerry West.

The Braves did not do anything to make Dantley's rookie season any easier. They sold forward Jim McMillian before the season to make room for the rookie in the lineup (increasing the pressure on him), then traded Bob McAdoo, also to the New York Knicks (causing opponents to center their attention on Dantley).

"They were saying, 'Let's see you replace McMillian, rookie,'" was the Buffalo fans' initial reaction, Dantley said. "But as soon as I got 15 points and 19 rebounds [in my first game] I stopped hearing about McMillian."

As for the effect of McAdoo's absence, Dantley said, "in college I was always playing against box-and-ones, and I hated them. Now I get double-teamed all the time. I beat my man and go to the hoop and there'll be another man waiting and I get called for the charge."

Nonetheless, Dantley connected on 52 per cent of his shots from the floor and 82 per cent of his free throws. He also had 587 rebounds.

"He is the real, true small forward," New York Nets Coach Kevin Loughery said. "He can hang in the air, fake, hesitate, change his shot and score. I've never seen anyone his size that strong. He's going to be a big star in this league. His only weak points are that he doesn't pass very well, doesn't pull up to shoot the jumper enough and he hasn't learned how to play defense on the bigger men."

He still may have some things to learn, but Dantley has proved he can be a big man in the NBA.

Although Dantley may have won the Rookie of the Year award, it would be hard to fault Houston Rockets Coach Tom Nissalke for making guard John Lucas the No. 1 pick of the college draft. Houston wanted the No. 1 choice badly enough to trade Joe Meriweather to Atlanta for it. Then, the Rockets made the rather surprising choice of Lucas.

"There never was a question in my mind," Nissalke said. There were a lot of fast guns in Houston, but no one willing or able to run things.

Lucas, a 6-3 product of the University of Maryland, had both the intelligence and the confidence to join a team of veterans and start giving orders, but in a manner which would not alienate his teammates.

"This kid came in yelling, 'Hey, big guys, hit the glass, get downcourt, I'll get you some dunkers,'" Houston forward Rudy Tomjanovich said.

"You can't get mad at him," said guard Mike Newlin, whose playing time was reduced a bit with Lucas' addition. "He has such a zest for life. Lucas doesn't overwhelm you with talent. He's just smooth. He asserted himself without infringing on anybody else's space, which is really an art."

"People just better be ready to play when they hit that floor with me," Lucas said. "I'm not going to score big in this league, or be spectacular. I'll have some bad games. But I know how to win. I've always been a leader since grade school."

The Rockets, who finished a game under .500 the previous season, won the Central Division title with a

49-33 record, the best in their history, thanks to Lucas' floor direction. He averaged 5.6 assists and 11.1 points a game.

The Rockets' selection of Lucas as the top pick was such a surprise because the college Player of the Year, Scott May, appeared such a can't-miss prospect. In leading Indiana to the NCAA championship, the 6-7 May demonstrated a mastery of all facets of the game.

But May, selected by the Chicago Bulls as the league's No. 2 choice, came down with mononucleosis early in training camp and missed the Bulls' first 10 regular season games. Consequently, the Bulls got off to a 2-14 start, but as May recovered his strength Chicago began to mesh as a team and won 20 of its last 24 games to make the playoffs. May finished with a 14.6 scoring average and grabbed six rebounds a game as he gave every indication of fulfilling his reputation.

North Carolina center Mitch Kupchak, 6-10, joined Dantley and May on the U.S. Olympic front line so many critics said was too small to win in foreign competition. The U.S. gold medal silenced those critics, but Kupchak still was regarded as suspect NBA material by many. Kupchak quickly convinced the Washington Bullets of his value as a reserve, but his late season performance suggests an even larger role is deserved.

Washington Coach Dick Motta said, "I envision Mitch developing into a Bob Pettit-type forward. He has the ability and the enthusiasm to be a great player. Kupchak is a 6-10 Jerry Sloan who can shoot."

Kupchak sank 57.2 per cent of his field goal attempts to finish second only to Kareem Abdul-Jabbar in the NBA, averaging 10.4 points a game. The Bullets also received a 7.8 points a game contribution from rookie guard Larry Wright.

In evaluating last season's rookies, though, Loughery gave an assessment most coaches would agree with: "Dantley may be the best rookie now, but if you're talking about potential it's Robert Parish."

Parish, a 7-footer from Centenary, led the Golden State Warriors in blocked shots with 94 and averaged 9.1 points a game coming off the bench.

Golden State Coach Al Attles said, "He can shoot, and when you find that talent in a center you can wait for improvement in other departments."

Other rookies to earn substantial playing time were Detroit center-forward Leon Douglas, Atlanta guard Armond Hill, Kansas City forward Richard Washington, Los Angeles swingman Earl Tatum, Milwaukee guard Quinn Buckner, Phoenix guard Ron Lee, Portland guard Johnny Davis and New York Knicks center-forward Lonnie Shelton.

Enthusiasm Regained

Maybe it's the high altitude. The thin air and the lack of oxygen, maybe that's what addles their brains. There must be some reason those basketball giants seem a mite off-the-wall, earning millions and hating it, complaining about the publicity, expressing a preference for factory work or jail, calling reporters' questions too superficial to dignify with an answer and then refusing to discuss important issues, complaining about being unloved, and so on, ad nauseam.

They're not all like that, it was said. There are some level-headed young men walking around in the rarified atmosphere. Well, there's one at least—Dave Cowens.

Then Dave Cowens got up and took a walk, just got up and excused himself from the Boston Celtics. The previous year the 6-foot-9 redhead had led the Celtics to the National Basketball Association championship in his usual commando style, but now he just did not feel like playing any more.

Walking out on a team is no longer unusual, basketball players having played a major role in making it fashionable. But it was no more expected from Cowens than it would be from Mr. Celtic, John Havlicek.

Cowens, whose bright red hair seems to be a warning of the fire that burns beneath, always had been one of the most intense players in the NBA, not the kind to jump ship. The modern basketball player is notorious for his fragile and overblown ego, in which a wrinkled uniform is taken as an indication of some dark vendetta by management and sufficient reason to storm out of the locker room. And many players have used going AWOL as a salary-negotiating tactic. But Cowens was a throwback to the old-time player who seemed to enjoy the game.

And that's why Cowens left the Celtics. He no longer was enjoying the game, so nine games into the 1976-77 season he quit.

"I just lost my enthusiasm for the game," he said at the time. "That's all I can say. This wasn't something sudden for me, I'd been thinking about it for three months. I even thought seriously about quitting before the season started, but I figured I'd just try it and see how it was. And then I just didn't have it. Nothing. When somebody drives right by you and you shrug your shoulders and say, 'Aw, what the hell,' when you go down and make a basket like a robot, when you win or lose a ball game and it doesn't matter either way, when you can't even get mad at the refs, then something's wrong."

Although a shameful amount of players seem to have exactly that attitude during the regular season, Cowens was not content to go through the motions and collect his $280,000 salary.

"When there's nothing left, there's no use making believe there is. I don't want to spoil the Celtics and I don't want to take their money if I'm not earning it," Cowens said in explanation. "I just quit my job, that's all. What's wrong with that? Other guys do it every day. Nobody makes a big thing out of them."

But other guys don't resurrect one of professional sports' greatest dynasties as Cowens had done with the Celtics. During his six years with Boston, Cowens had led the Celtics to a pair of NBA titles and had won the league's Most Valuable Player award in 1973.

As is the case with so many pro athletes, Cowens is unable to understand his dreams and aspirations are not his own. They are shared by all the Celtic fans, who live vicariously through the exploits of "their team." The fan who is pushed around all day at his job finally wins one when he sits back, beer in hand, and watches the Celtics demolish another opponent. Consequently, Cowens' life is not his own, although he is well compensated for the intrusion.

If Cowens expected a surcease in the media coverage surrounding his life, the "retirement" brought the opposite reaction. He was in the spotlight more than ever.

Boston General Manager Red Auerbach had treaded delicately with Cowens from the moment the 28-year-old center announced his intentions of leaving the Celtics. Careful never to push too much or come on too strong, Auerbach persisted in the art of gentle persuasion and, after a 60-day vacation, finally brought the hesitant Cowens back into the Celtic fold.

Cowens admitted the constant attention of the media, one of the aspects of basketball he finds most disagreeable, affected his decision to return to the Celtics.

"Everything gets distorted whether I'm playing or not playing," he said. "So I might as well play instead of always explaining why I'm not playing."

At the same time, Cowens gave an indication of the

emotional and mental turmoil he had suffered in making and living with his decision.

"I believe I did the right thing," he said. "The worst thing in the world is to be confused. When I was confused I had to make a decision. What I did was selfish, but I couldn't think of any other way. I may look back five years from now and say, 'Boy, that was about the dumbest thing you've ever done.'"

But, having made a conscious decision to play basketball, he returned with the old zeal and aggressiveness and again led the Celtics into the playoffs.

Despite missing 30 games, which cost him $102,000 in salary, Cowens was the fifth leading Celtic in minutes played. He finished with a 16.4 scoring average and grabbed 697 rebounds, an average of 13.9 which would have placed him second in the league, if he had fulfilled the minimum requirements.

After the Celtics swept past the San Antonio Spurs in the opening round of the playoffs, Cowens was chiefly responsible for taking Philadelphia to the limit before the 76ers finally ousted Boston.

With the season concluded, Cowens at last was left in privacy to enjoy his latest avocation. Basketball is Dave Cowens' job, so for sport he drives a taxicab around Boston.

It pays a shade less than $280,000 a year, but it affords Cowens the solitude he craves. That's something his money can't buy.

An Embarrassment of Riches

For years Julius Erving's basketball magic had been deprecated by comments such as "Yeah, but look who he's playing against. How would he do in the NBA?"

Well, the merger between the American Basketball Association and the National Basketball Association proved to be the embarrassment so many had predicted. Good grief, talk about overrated—mint juleps, Cher's looks, Reggie Jackson's self opinion, the Baltimore Colts in Super Bowl III—and the NBA deserves to be at the top of the list. Considering how rotten so many NBA owners had said the caliber of ball in the ABA was, they should be reported to the Environmental Protection Agency for fouling the air with their own brand of basketball.

Four ABA survivors were welcomed in the NBA, as long as each brought along $3.2-million for the privilege of mixing with their social betters. The other two ABA clubs, the Kentucky Colonels and the Spirits of St. Louis, were disbanded and their personnel, inferior though it may have been, was divided among the NBA clubs. And, just to show how willing they were to upgrade the caliber of those poor ABA teams, the newcomers were not allowed to sign any college players other than free agents.

Then, this invasion of second-rate players managed to restructure the balance of power in the NBA.

Where would the NBA champion Portland Trail Blazers be without Maurice Lucas and Dave Twardzik? Still trying to convince Bill Walton he won't make it in the pros until he changes his diet, that's where.

Imagine the Philadelphia 76ers without ABA players.

The ABA players noticed some differences in the NBA, such as non-stop flights to their destinations, people in the stands and better playing facilities.

But Lucas articulated the best aspect of life in the NBA. "I feel a lot more comfortable and secure," the Portland forward said. "I don't have to run to the bank as soon as I get my check."

Even Seattle backup center Mike Green looked favorably upon that aspect. Asked about the thrill of finally playing in the NBA, Green challenged, "What do you think the NBA is—heaven? There's too much jamming the middle here. Guys spend half their lives learning how to play the game and then they can't use anything because it's all jammed up."

Asked if there wasn't something better about the NBA, Green admitted, "Yeah, in this league I get paid."

However, at the end of the season, the Indiana Pacers were on the brink of defaulting on their players' contracts because of the heavy indemnity payments to the NBA.

Generally, though, most players coming into the dream league felt the same as Denver's Bobby Jones, who immediately established himself as one of the top defensive forwards in the NBA.

"I really didn't experience much of a transition at all," he said. "It was basically the same. The toughest

AN EMBARRASSMENT OF RICHES

people I was guarding were from the ABA—Maurice Lucas, Julius Erving and Larry Kenon."

Lucas, a 6-9 forward from the Kentucky Colonels, proved to be just the help Walton needed up front to challenge Kareem Abdul-Jabbar for recognition as the league's top center. Walton led the league in rebounding with an average of 14.4 a game and Lucas was ninth with an 11.4 average. This board strength was responsible for the Trail Blazers developing possibly the best fast break in basketball.

Lucas also led the Trail Blazers in scoring with a 20.2 average, connecting on 47 per cent of his shots from the floor. Most important, with matchups such a vital part of basketball, Lucas proved to be the key in Portland's playoff victory over the Los Angeles Lakers, who had won the Pacific Division title by four games over the Trail Blazers in the regular season. The Lakers, whose 53-29 regular season record was the best in the NBA, did not have a forward capable of stopping Lucas. So when Abdul-Jabbar and Walton battled each other on more or less even terms, Lucas proved the big difference between the two teams as the Blazers gained the finals against the 76ers.

Twardzik is the guy who really should be doing those American Express commercials.

"Thank you Mrs. Twardzik . . . no, it's not Yul Brynner . . . that's two down and eight to go . . . we'll give you a hint, it's a basketball player . . . no, it's not Rick Barry . . . that's three down and seven to go."

Eventually, his mother might guess who Dave Twardzik is, but the rest of the world seems incapable of recognizing his talents. In the ABA, Twardzik labored for the Virginia Squires—and that's chain gang labor—without making much of an impression. He made the All-Star team, but even in the ABA they looked down upon him and figured someone had to represent the Squires.

In the dispersal draft, Twardzik was not exactly the most coveted player and there was no tremendous battle for the rights to sign him. Portland certainly got its money's worth, though, as Twardzik averaged 10.3 points a game and repeatedly drove the middle to set up Walton and Lucas for easy shots. Twardzik, who was fifth on the Blazers in playing time, sank 61.2 per cent of his field goal attempts, which would have led the league if he had met the minimum requirements. Twardzik connected on 263 shots, but the league requires a minimum of 300 to qualify for the league title. He also was second on the Blazers in assists with 247 and second in steals with 128.

Despite their outstanding seasons, Lucas and Twardzik might have gone completely unnoticed if Portland had not won the NBA championship because the controversial Walton receives so much attention.

"If I had this kind of year in New York, I'd be governor," Lucas said. And he's probably right.

Erving, the legendary Dr. J, was the catalyst to the merger between the NBA and the ABA. The NBA owners were given a strong shove toward a merger agreement by the Columbia Broadcasting System, which televises the NBA games. In the television contract negotiated last year, there were a few million extra dollars floating around in the small print on the condition there would be a merger. CBS officials were not shy about disclosing the cause of their merger concern. If they were going to televise pro basketball, they wanted the star of the show—Dr. J.

They got what they paid for and, yet, they didn't. On the New York Nets, Erving was the top banana. But the Nets acquired Tiny Archibald from the Kansas

City Kings and gave him top billing on the payroll ledger. Erving demanded more money and was sent packing to the 76ers in exchange for $3-million. Dr. J then signed a contract for another $3.5-million to complete the transaction. With all that money, Erving should have bought a basketball because too many of his teammates didn't want to part with the one being used in the game.

Erving got the ball often enough to lead the 76ers in scoring with a 21.6 average, connecting on 50 per cent of his field goal attempts. He had 695 rebounds to rank second to George McGinnis in that category and also was second in assists, steals and blocked shots.

"There's only one basketball player I'd pay to see and that's Julius Erving," former 76ers forward Billy Cunningham said.

"He's one of the greatest basketball players your eyes will ever witness," Philadelphia Coach Gene Shue said.

But Kevin Loughery, Erving's coach with the New York Nets, insisted throughout the regular season Erving had yet to display his full range of talents. It was during the playoffs that Erving proved Loughery right. While the rest of the 76ers, except Doug Collins, seemed able to do nothing right, Erving was a one-man gang before finally being overwhelmed by the Trail Blazers.

George McGinnis, who beat his ABA compatriots into the NBA by a year, was the 76er most guilty of collapsing in the playoffs. But the muscular forward had an outstanding regular season, averaging 21.4 points and 11.5 rebounds a game, and was selected as the 76ers' most valuable player by the Philadelphia writers. Long and lean Caldwell Jones, a 6-11 ex-ABA center, also made a significant contribution to the 76ers' Atlantic Division title.

Artis Gilmore, the first choice in the dispersal draft, took some time to get acclimated to the NBA and the Chicago Bulls, but eventually he led a late-season surge into the playoffs. The 7-foot-2 center averaged 18.6 points and 13 rebounds, fourth best in the league. After a horrible start, which included a 13-game losing streak, the Bulls won 20 of their last 24 regular season games to finish second in the Midwest Division with a 44-38 record.

The Detroit Pistons, who tied the Bulls for second with an identical record, received an unexpected boost from M.L. Carr, who averaged 13.3 points a game and had 631 rebounds. Unfortunately, the highly talented Marvin Barnes proved more adept at raising hell than uplifting the Pistons' fortunes. Between run-ins with management and the law, the 6-9 Barnes averaged 9.3 points and five rebounds a game. Ralph Simpson, though, averaged 11 points a game after being acquired from the Denver Nuggets.

Undoubtedly, the most dramatic influence a single ABA player had on his new club was Moses Malone's effect on the Houston Rockets, who shot from perennial also-ran to the Central Division title. The 23-year-old, 6-11 Malone broke the NBA single season record for offensive rebounds with 437, easily surpassing Paul Silas' mark of 365. The Trail Blazers made Malone the fifth selection of the dispersal draft, but traded him to the Buffalo Braves before the season began. The Braves used Malone for only six minutes in two games before shipping him to the Rockets. His imposing presence under the boards turned Houston from a team which finished one game under .500 to the division champs with a 49-33 record.

The Kansas City Kings pulled one of the best backcourts in basketball out of the ABA by picking Ron Boone in the dispersal draft and acquiring Brian Taylor from the Nets. Boone led the Kings in scoring with a 22.2 average and Taylor, since traded to the Denver Nuggets, was second with a 17-point average. Taylor was second in the league in steals, averaging 2.76.

The Milwaukee Bucks landed the league's seventh leading rebounder in Swen Nater, who since has been traded to Buffalo. The Los Angeles Lakers added a valuable backcourt performer in Don Chaney, who had jumped to the ABA from the Boston Celtics.

As for the four ABA teams accepted into the NBA, they all acquitted themselves quite well, even the New York Nets, who had their heart torn out before the season began.

The Denver Nuggets figured to be the strongest of the four newcomers and fulfilled those expectations with a 50-32 record for the Midwest Division championship. The San Antonio Spurs, an unheralded squad, also qualified for the playoffs with a 44-38 record in their first NBA season.

The Nuggets, an awesome team at home as their 36-5 record attests, introduced a couple of new stars to the NBA. David Thompson, despite his 6-3 height, was every bit as awesome as he had been in college and the ABA. And Bobby Jones, the working man's forward, convinced many observers he was the league's best defensive forward since Dave DeBusschere.

Thompson, who started the season at guard and then switched to his more familiar post at forward, was the league's fourth leading scorer with 25.9 points a game. Teammate Dan Issel, who created quite a stir when Denver fans stuffed the ballot box to make him the Western Conference's starting center in the All-Star game instead of Abdul-Jabbar, was 10th with a 22.3 average. Jones, who was sixth in steals with an average of 2.27, also continued to demonstrate his offensive prowess. Jones, who never seems to take a bad shot and led the ABA in field goal percentage during his two years in the league, was the NBA's third leading percentage shooter with an accuracy mark of .570 in averaging 15.1 points a game.

The Spurs came into the NBA as the most anonymous of the four ABA clubs and made the playoffs easily, despite the fact their top guard, James Silas, was injured and played in only 22 games. The smooth 6-foot-7 George Gervin was shifted to the backcourt and finished ninth in scoring with a 23.1 average and fourth in field goal percentage at .544. Larry Kenon, a deceptively strong 6-9 forward, was 12th in scoring with a 21.9 mark and 10th in rebounds with an average of 11.3 a game. Underrated center Billy Paultz, who fools a lot of people with his Pillsbury doughboy appearance, averaged 15.6 points a game and was the league's ninth leading shot blocker with an average of 2.06 a game. Guard Mike Gale was fifth in the league in steals with a 2.33 average.

Especially adept at run-and-gun basketball, the Spurs proved to be the 76ers' toughest nemesis by beating Philadelphia in three out of their four meetings—and beating them badly.

Coming into the season, the Indiana Pacers appeared the weakest team in the NBA and the loss of center Len Elmore for the season did not make matters look any better. But Coach Bob Leonard did a superb job in directing the Pacers to a 36-46 record.

Forward Billy Knight, playing out of position half the season, was the league's second leading scorer with a 26.6 average. But everyone already was aware Knight was a great scoring machine. It was guard Don Buse who caught everyone by surprise. Buse, who led the league in assists and steals, went from being a nonentity to the most coveted guard in the league. Buse averaged 8.5 assists and 3.47 steals a game. Second-year forward Dan Roundfield improved dramatically with a 13.9 scoring average and was the NBA's eighth leading shot blocker, often filling in at center.

The Nets finished with the NBA's worst record, 22-60, but much worse was expected after Erving was sent to Philadelphia at the beginning of the season and Tiny Archibald was sidelined for the season after only 34 games. Loughery did a masterful job of coaching just to get his crew of castoffs 22 victories.

At the conclusion of the season, the four ABA clubs had earned the respect of their NBA rivals and the fans. Thompson was selected to the league's first All-Star team and Erving, McGinnis and Gervin were second-team selections.

The only persons eating crow at the season's end were those NBA officials who had spent so much time downgrading the quality of the ABA.

At Home in Houston

And Moses came down, not from the mountain but from Buffalo, to lead them out of the wilderness.

Three years ago, Moses Malone had been such a hot prospect the Utah Stars of the American Basketball Association were willing to shell out more than a million dollars for his basketball talents, although they had been tested only on the high school level.

His first season with the Stars had been surprisingly successful, but his second pro season was one of injury and terminal illness. Malone was injured, but he would recover. The American Basketball Association was dying and there would be no miraculous recovery.

The Stars beat the rest of the ABA into the grave, so Malone's contract was transferred to the Spirits of St. Louis. When the four strongest members of the ABA merged with the National Basketball Association, Malone and his compatriots on the folding clubs were placed in a dispersal draft for the established NBA teams.

Portland managed to land Maurice Lucas and Malone in the dispersal draft, leaving the Trail Blazers with an embarrassing wealth of big men, what with Bill Walton and Sidney Wicks already on the roster. The names looked great on paper, except in the financial ledger. Consequently, the Trail Blazers lightened the payroll by sending Malone to Buffalo.

But Malone wasn't even in Buffalo long enough to get frostbite before the Braves passed him on to Houston. The 22-year-old vagabond was reunited in Houston with Tom Nissalke, his coach at Utah, and John Lucas, his friend from his "almost" college career.

The 6-foot-11 Malone was only 14 years old when the college recruiters began pounding down the door of his small home in Petersburg, Va. Living with his mother on an income of slightly more than $5,000 a year, Malone was overwhelmed by the dreams of riches conjured up by college recruiters.

For four years, Malone was stalked constantly by the recruiters. Malone averaged 35.8 points and 25 rebounds a game during his senior year of high school as the recruiting pressure intensified. During the ABA's college draft, the Utah Stars made Malone their third-round choice, but the fact was forgotten as soon as the University of Maryland won the Moses sweepstakes.

Then, just before Malone was to start classes at Maryland, the Stars came forward with an offer too good to be refused.

Maryland Coach Lefty Driesell fought a good battle, getting Malone to delay his decision until a lawyer had examined the contract for him. During the wait, Driesell got Malone to come to College Park for a walk around campus, and his guide was Lucas.

Eventually, though, Malone had to take the money. At the New York press conference announcing his signing, Malone had little to say and looked extremely uncomfortable, mumbling the shortest possible answers in response to reporters' questions. "I just want to be happy," he said.

However, happiness is tough to find when a shy, introverted boy painfully lacking in social assuredness is suddenly thrust into a life of fast living and super egos. The culture shock from small town life to the life of a pro basketball player was great, and Malone found it difficult to feel comfortable, especially in the company of teammates decades older socially. And, once he started to grow accustomed to his teammates, it was off to another city.

In Houston, though, it was easier to be happy. He had a coach who really wanted him. But, more important, he had a friend.

Lucas possesses all the social graces Malone lacks. The son of high school principals, Lucas brims with self-confidence. He is articulate and exudes an aura of self-assuredness, evidenced by his coming in as a rookie and becoming the floor leader of the Rockets.

Lucas quickly went to work building Malone's ego, had the bashful giant move into an apartment above his own and constantly castigated Moses for mumbling. Lucas wasted no opportunity to publicize Malone as the greatest offensive rebounder in basketball. By the season's conclusion, the NBA statistics agreed.

Malone crashed the offensive boards for 437 rebounds, smashing the league record of 365 held by Paul Silas. This statistic was the prime reason the Rockets were transformed from a team which finished one game under .500 in 1975-76 to the Central Division champions with a 49-33 record in 1976-77.

"Malone's offensive rebounding means an extra eight to 10 points a game for us," guard Mike Newlin said.

"You can talk about all the great offensive rebounders in the game, but I've never seen one better than this man," added forward Rudy Tomjanovich.

Nissalke, of course, appeared a genius after leading the Rockets to their most successful season. The Rockets traded for the first pick in the college draft and made Lucas, a guard, their rather surprising choice. Then, Nissalke went after Malone.

"I knew what Moses could do because I coached him at Utah," the outspoken Nissalke said. "He's not a fundamentally sound player yet and he's limited in what he can do offensively, but he's a great natural rebounder and he's eager to learn."

Malone's learning process should not be taken too lightly. After all, he still should be playing college ball, so there's room for improvement.

"We hope to work with him this summer on developing a couple of more moves inside and he should be 25 per cent better next season," Nissalke said, following the successful 1976-77 campaign.

The 23-year-old Malone, who played only six minutes with Buffalo before being traded to the Rockets, averaged 13.5 points and 13.4 rebounds a game for Houston. He was the league's third leading rebounder behind Walton and Los Angeles' Kareem Abdul-Jabbar.

Malone played an even larger role in getting the Rockets past the Washington Bullets in the quarterfinals of the NBA playoffs. He averaged 19.5 points, 17 rebounds and two blocked shots a game against the Bullets. That carried the Rockets into the semifinals against Philadelphia, but the 76ers proved a bit better than Houston.

However, a happy and maturing Malone should only get better, a prospect to be savored by Houston fans.

Computer's Choice

As dependent as a computer may be on the human hand which feeds it, the hunk of inanimate machinery often has a mind of its own, so to speak, when it comes to making a decision.

Let people select the NBA's Most Valuable Player, and the perennial choice is Kareem Abdul-Jabbar. Ask a fan who is the most exciting player to watch, and inevitably the answer is Julius Erving. You want to know the scoring champion, all you have to do is look at the statistics.

But ask a computer, which has never so much as seen a game, to determine the most complete player in the league, and you're letting yourself in for a shock. A computer was asked to do this recently for the 1976-77 season and, digesting only the facts without allowing a degree of emotion to filter in, came up with quite a revelation.

Bobby Jones of the Denver Nuggets, whose common name and unassuming personality stamp him as "Mr. Anonymous" to many fans around the country, was judged to be the "most consistent and most productive" player in the NBA.

Surprised? So was Bobby Jones, who has trouble

gaining attention on his own team, which last year included David Thompson, Dan Issel and Marvin Webster.

"Yeah, I was surprised," admitted the forthright forward. "I didn't think there was any way I would win."

Yet, the hard, unemotional facts showed that Jones led Abdul-Jabbar, the runnerup, in five of the seven categories upon which the ratings are based. Abdul-Jabbar, the official MVP for the fifth time in seven years, outdistanced Jones in scoring and rebounding, but Jones was superior in assists, field goal percentage, free throw percentage, steals and blocked shots.

"I really had my best year as far as overall categories," Jones said. "And while I was playing less and trying to produce as much as I could in that time, Kareem's a little more of a floor leader. Even when he's not scoring he's on the court, doing other things and building confidence in his team just by being there."

Perhaps it took a machine to emphasize what a thoroughly complete player Jones is. Although he averaged only 29½ minutes per game, Jones ranked third on the Nuggets in scoring (15.1 points), second in rebounds (678), first in steals (186), blocked shots (162) and field goal percentage (.570), and fourth in assists (264). In addition, he was the leading vote-getter on the All-Defensive team, all of which prompted Chicago Coach Ed Badger to proclaim Jones "the most complete forward I've ever seen."

"I feel I have an advantage over the others by not playing as much," Jones said in explanation of his performance. "I'm a little more intense as far as output of energy goes. I know I'm not going to put in a full game, and I pattern myself to the point where I expend all my energy to the limited time."

BOBBY JONES

If it still comes as a surprise to you that a guy named Bobby Jones was judged to be the most complete player in the NBA, a couple of other insights into the big guy might startle you. The first is that he took his award money, every penny of the $10,000, and gave it away. And the second revelation is that Jones has accomplished what he has despite a heart irregularity.

A deeply religious young man from Charlotte, N.C., the 26-year-old Jones gave the money awarded to him by Seagram's Seven Crowns of Sports to various Christian groups and to Brad Hoffman, a former teammate at the University of North Carolina. Hoffman's wife had given birth to twins prematurely and their medical bills were costly.

"I just felt first of all that God gave me this talent I have and the ability to play this game for a purpose," Jones explained self-consciously, "I felt part of the purpose is to win money and give it away. I felt it wasn't mine to keep. My body is the holy temple of the Lord, and I felt I could not use that money in any way but to help others."

Jones, who does not touch alcohol, said he wasn't sure if his actions would have been the same had the money come from other than a whisky manufacturer.

"I decided when I won the monthly award that if I won the whole thing I would give the money to the Lord, because He gave me the ability," Jones said. "I really feel like I haven't had to work that hard for it."

As for the heart problem, Jones first suspected trouble when he would feel fatigue and experience difficulty breathing during games. Yet, during his first two years with the Nuggets, when they still were in the ABA, he missed only one game.

In the summer of 1976, Jones went to a doctor for

extensive tests, at which time the problem was traced to his heart.

"At first they thought I had a loose valve or a two-way valve," Jones said, "but they couldn't find one so they performed other tests. The doctors explained that a heart has one primary pacemaker and six secondary pacemakers, and when I exercised one of the secondary pacemakers was taking over.

"They gave me something to put my heart pacemaker, my natural one, under control so the number of beats can be regulated in a natural way without fluttering, and it would go up naturally as I exercised. All it amounted to was that my pacemaker had a slight irregularity."

Jones emphasizes that there is no real problem with his heart, and this has nothing to do with the fact he sat on the bench an average of 18½ minutes a game last season.

"The heart doesn't affect my stamina or anything like that," he said. "Basically, Larry [Coach Larry Brown] was trying to play everybody a little less to get ready for the playoffs. He didn't want the team to wear down like it had in previous years. We have so much talent, everybody was given a lot of time."

Indeed, only Thompson and Issel saw more playing time with Denver than Jones, and in Issel's case it amounted to only 88 minutes more.

"I wasn't unhappy with my situation," Jones stated. "I was very satisfied with the time I got. I don't really care if I get more this season. It's just a matter of how I can help the team."

Brown feels one way Jones can help the team is by adding bulk to his 6-9, 212-pound frame, a suggestion Bobby doesn't particularly cherish. "I might try to put on a few pounds, but that's the weight I feel comfortable at," he said. "I have a lot of quickness, and that's my main concern. He [Brown] feels with more weight I'll be more of a factor under the boards. He's the coach and he has the interest of the team at heart."

Although he doesn't have the flair of other power forwards such as Erving, George McGinnis, Maurice Lucas and Larry Kenon, Jones is well respected and deeply feared by rival players.

"The guy is one of the best defensive players I've ever seen," marveled Bill Bradley before he retired from the Knicks. "He's very unselfish, a great competitor, always knows where the ball is, can really rebound and is a very good passer. In many respects I'd say he's their key player."

Brown said of Jones, "He doesn't play with the ball like Julius Erving. He sneaks up on you and before you know it he's got 15 points and rebounds. The average fan may not realize he's in the game."

All well and good. But Bobby, don't you want to be fawned over by the fans? Don't you feel, well, anonymous?

"I don't really know, I don't know or care. I had a lot of publicity from my high school days, mostly locally, some nationally, and it's not that I'm tired of it, I never really pursued it or wanted it. I don't care about it. My game isn't really that spectacular. I do the job they're paying me for."

With such a common name, a religious background and a desire only to blend quietly with the general team effort, you get the feeling Bobby Jones might remain Mr. Anonymous even if he gave away $10,000 every week.

Blessedly, there's this sharp little computer that thinks otherwise.

Unhappiness at the Top

For millions of American boys, a career as a professional basketball player rates a close second to being king of the world. It's a dream job, particularly to poor kids, representing the opportunity for them to become instant millionaires, national celebrities and globetrotting bon vivants.

They perform on television several nights a week, have the nation's leading sportswriters coaxing them for words of wisdom, are fawned on by adoring, wide-eyed fans and have the golden chance to take advantage of their status and set themselves up for future careers in other lucrative fields.

These big dudes have it made, yet suddenly they want to give it all up. And many of those who stay behind only want to fight, whether it be with teammate, rival player or referee. And even the wives are joining the fray with inflammatory newspaper articles.

What's going on here, anyway?

Dave Cowens, the intense, withdrawn center of the Boston Celtics, touched off the bizarre chain of events that mystified fans last season when he took a "leave of absence" early in November. In turn, Pete Maravich of the New Orleans Jazz, Bob Lanier of the Detroit

Pistons and Jamaal Wilkes of the Golden State Warriors—all of them high-paid stars—announced that they too were considering immediate retirement.

Cowens, of course, is the only one who followed through. Giving up all claim to his $250,000-a-year salary during his leave, the 28-year-old redhead said he couldn't continue because he lost his enthusiasm for the game and he felt stale.

Just as suddenly, two months later, Cowens returned, saying he intended to remain "forevermore."

"A lot of things have happened to me over the course of not playing that I felt it was better to play," he explained. "People were following me around, seeing what I'm doing. So I'm just going to play basketball again. It's easier."

In a rare moment when he allowed an outsider to share his emotions, Cowens stated, "I think what I did was a selfish thing. But the worst thing in the world is to be confused all the time. So I made my decision and I'll live with it. Maybe in five years I'll say, 'That was the dumbest thing you have ever done,' but I doubt it."

Returning to work, Cowens appeared in 50 games for the Celtics, averaging 16.4 points and totaling 697 rebounds.

Soon after Cowens walked off the court and tried to find anonymity in the crowd, Maravich revealed that he was toying with the thought of forsaking the game that was paying him some $450,000 annually.

"Dave Cowens did what I had been thinking about doing for some time now," Pistol Pete said. "It's funny in a way, because Dave beat me to the punch." Trying to rationalize his position, Maravich added, "I was shooting about 20 per cent and I saw no light at the end of the tunnel in the first seven or eight games. To play this game night after night, to get beat up and have your ankles broken and teeth knocked out, you wonder, 'Why am I here?' "

Despite this poor mental attitude, Maravich led the NBA in scoring with a 31.1 average, making him only the fifth guard ever to lead the league. But for the sixth time in seven years as a pro, Maravich played with a losing team, a situation that still may prompt him toward an early retirement.

"Everybody has a stigma about certain people," he stated. "When you're on a losing team, you're a loser. When you're on a winning team, then you're the greatest thing going. I think some people are destined to become losers and some people are destined to become winners. Sometimes I feel that maybe I'm destined never to win an NBA championship."

Lanier also was tired when he spoke in December of taking a leave of absence. Whereas Cowens was tired of being on public display and Maravich was tired of losing, Lanier grew weary of the constant fighting by his teammates, compounded by a series of injuries he suffered.

"Right now I'm just mentally tired," said the 6-11, 255-pound center. "There are lots of pressures and lots of headaches in this game. I'm going to talk the whole thing over with my wife, and then do whatever I have to do. I might sit out."

Then, referring to the dissension that plagued the Pistons all year, he said, "They are internal problems, not things I want to talk about in public. I hope they can be worked out. But it's hard to play in all this turmoil and right now I'm really getting nervous. My eyes are starting to twitch from nerves, and right now I'm about at the point where I just might take a rest, just like Cowens. That's how serious the situation is."

The previous year, Lanier had suffered a broken collarbone, spine injury and tendinitis in both elbows. He continued on with the Pistons last season, only to break his right hand March 4. After sitting out 15 games, he returned to the lineup as Detroit wound up a disappointing campaign, although individually he performed well with a 25.3 scoring average.

If you're wondering about any correlation among the three, consider that Cowens, Maravich and Lanier all were 28 in their winter of unhappiness, with Cowens' and Lanier's birth dates falling within 15 days of each other. All were in their seventh year in the NBA.

But the seeds of unrest weren't limited to that age category. Jamaal Wilkes was a mere 23, only two years removed from being voted the NBA's Rookie of the Year, when he, too, revealed that he was contemplating retirement. Unlike Cowens, he wasn't prepared to quit in mid-season, but like the Celtic center he feels the compensations aren't worth the demands made on his life.

"People only relate to me as a symbol, not a person," he explained. "I understand that, but I don't have to like it. You can't escape it, even when you're shopping or eating. The road trips, the length of the season, they all restrict you. I want to feel my way for a while before making a decision whether I want to continue playing.

"But I'm very serious about quitting. It didn't surprise me at all when Cowens said he was leaving. There are a lot of sensitive people who play this game. A lot of individuals can't do anything else while others can. I know I can do other things. Everybody will have to decide what's best for him, and some of the things that develop will probably shake up some people.

"Other ballplayers in all sports have probably gone

through the same thing and maybe it's only recently, with salaries being high and other opportunities opening up, that a player can seriously consider quitting at an early age to do what he considers more important to him. Maybe 10 years ago, a player in my situation would have felt that he had no choice but to continue playing. But I've got a choice."

One choice Wilkes had was to play out his option with Golden State. He did just that, and signed with the Los Angeles Lakers. He was encouraged to return to LA by a fellow UCLA alumnus, Kareem Abdul-Jabbar. The man Wilkes has to beat out for the small forward job on the Lakers is Cazzie Russell, who had taken the same free agent route south three years before.

As salaries have leapfrogged to such insane proportions, temperaments have soared to explosive levels. Perhaps, with dissension now a staple ingredient on most teams, it isn't so surprising that sensitive young men still in their prime would consider giving up a job that earns them hundreds of thousands of dollars a year.

Individual personalities are changing under this intensely competitive situation. Two years ago, for example, Slick Watts requested a clause in his contract with Seattle stipulating that if management felt his play was below expectation, it could withhold part of his salary. "I don't want money for nothing," Watts said. "I just want what I work for."

Last season, this same Slick Watts asked to be traded because he wasn't satisfied with his salary. "I'm concerned with getting paid more," he said. "I've got to get what I'm worth."

Have another example: For nine years, Walt Frazier of the New York Knicks was about the easiest gentleman in the game to talk to. He was a favorite of writers and fans, and his public image was enviable. Then trouble came to him and his team, and Frazier gave up his captaincy and let it be known he no longer was readily available to the media.

"I'm just tired of people asking, 'What's wrong with Walt Frazier?' I'm tired of being blamed for everything that goes wrong," he said. "I'm not talking because I don't want to be misquoted anymore."

If Frazier wasn't talking, it seems everyone else was, including the wives of Julius Erving and Bob McAdoo. Turquoise Erving authored an article in *The New York Times* in which she said, among other things, "No one here respects Shue [Philadelphia Coach Gene Shue]," and Brenda McAdoo wrote a letter to a Buffalo paper deploring the way the Braves' fans were treating their former hero since his trade to the Knicks.

Meantime, on the court and off, among teammates and rivals, fights are becoming commonplace. Some of the memorable matchups last season included: Lanier vs. Jim Eakins, Kareem Abdul-Jabbar vs. Tom Burleson, Marvin Barnes vs. Mike Bantom, Sidney Wicks vs. Rick Barry, Kevin Porter vs. Jack Marin, Mel Davis vs. Dean Tolson, and Swen Nater vs. Lonnie Shelton.

The one that drew the most attention, of course, occurred in the second game of the championship series when two behemoths, Maurice Lucas and Darryl Dawkins, squared off. Each was fined $2500.

The restlessness that affected players and management also reached the referees, who went on strike the closing day of the season and remained out for the early rounds of the playoffs, which were worked by pickups.

What's going on here?

One man who feels he knows the answer is Red Auerbach, who won nine NBA championships in the 16 years he coached the Celtics. In an article he wrote for *The Times,* Auerbach said, "By and large, we're seeing an erosion of basic values—things like pride and integrity and dedication."

Auerbach, who now is president and general manager of the Celtics, added, "Now, some kids are guaranteed lifetime security before they do anything to help their clubs. That's ridiculous. We've created a system that works against motivation, desire and discipline."

Knicks and Knocks

Bob McAdoo is an exceptional ball player and his one-year career at the University of North Carolina proved it. The 6-10 McAdoo, who went to Vincennes Junior College, was recruited by North Carolina Coach Dean Smith, who does not like to take transfer students. But, for McAdoo, he was willing to make an exception.

After one season with the Tar Heels, McAdoo had the pros drooling over his great shooting touch. He would have been the No. 1 pick of the draft, but it had been rumored he already had signed with the Virginia Squires of the American Basketball Association. Still, the Trail Blazers, who had the first choice, were entertaining McAdoo in Portland prior to the draft. Then, just before the draft, NBA Commissioner Walter Kennedy announced McAdoo definitely had signed with the Squires.

The Trail Blazers then decided to make 6-11 LaRue Martin of Loyola of Chicago their No. 1 pick. However, Buffalo Braves owner Paul Snyder was not dissuaded and picked McAdoo anyway. He then tenaciously negotiated a settlement with the Squires, who could be induced to part with any player for the right price.

Snyder was willing to pay this untested rookie

$350,000 annually for five years. But, when McAdoo justified Snyder's extravagance, the Braves owner decided he would cost too much to sign once the original five-year contract had expired.

So last fall Snyder placed McAdoo on the block and the New York Knicks were tripping over their wallets, they were in such a hurry.

The deal became a comedy of errors, though, when Snyder began dealing McAdoo to the Knicks at the same time his partner John Brown was arranging to send the high-scoring center to the Seattle SuperSonics. Deals with both clubs were settled before Snyder and Brown discovered what the other was doing. And when Snyder finally had McAdoo ready for shipping, the Braves owner threw a last-minute monkey wrench into the deal by insisting the Knicks also take forward Tom McMillen and his hefty salary.

Once again the trade was stalled, but the Knicks were so eager to obtain McAdoo they added McMillen to the payroll. The Braves, in exchange, received John Gianelli and $3-million and there never was any doubt which was the most important ingredient in the deal.

As it turned out, McMillen more than lived up to the Knicks' expectations, proving a valuable reserve.

But there was virtually no way McAdoo could fulfill the Knicks' hopes. The squad had grown old and some poor draft selections had not provided replacements for the Knicks' retiring stars, so they were sinking steadily in the Atlantic Division.

The last No. 1 draft choice to make it big was Walt Frazier in 1967. After Frazier came Bill Hosket, John Warren, Mike Price, Dean Meminger, Tom Riker, Mel Davis and Eugene Short. Consequently, the Knicks were seeking to buy their way back to respectability. They had spent a fortune in 1975 trying to lure George

McGinnis away from the Indiana Pacers, ignoring the fact the Philadelphia 76ers held the NBA rights to McGinnis. However, Commissioner Larry O'Brien voided the contract and the little adventure cost the Knicks their first-round choice in the 1976 draft.

The Knicks were more than willing to take Spencer Haywood and his expensive contract off the Sonics' hands. But the Knicks continued to lose, so they went to work at adding a top-caliber center, something they had not had since Willis Reed retired. Consequently, when McAdoo was put on the market, the Knicks were not going to be outbid, figuring this was all that was needed to win the NBA championship.

But, even with names like McAdoo, Haywood, Monroe and Frazier in the lineup, the Knicks could not qualify for the playoffs, finishing with a 40-42 record. With all those great shooters, the Knicks had the best field goal percentage in the league. All those great shooters, though, simply let loose from the outside, so the Knicks were by far the NBA's worst team for offensive rebounds, getting only 974. Phoenix, the worst all-around rebounding team in the league after two of its starting forwards were injured and missed half the season, was next at 1059.

McAdoo, the 26-year-old center who had won three straight NBA scoring titles and one Most Valuable Player Award, averaged 26.7 points a game for the Knicks to finish with a 25.8 mark, the fifth best in the league.

For years, McAdoo has been rankled by what he considers a lack of recognition for his achievements. His trade to New York certainly appeared to take care of that problem, athletes in the Big Apple not lacking in publicity.

But, as the Knicks struggled to make the playoffs

and then failed, media attention focused on what's wrong with the Knicks and McAdoo.

He still displayed the same great touch with his one-handed jump shot and the same outstanding quickness for a big man, but suddenly these assets almost became a liability in the eyes of the Knicks' critics.

The rap against McAdoo was that he shoots too much; that he's not a team player. In Buffalo, it had always been a case of the Braves not winning despite his marvelous talents. In the glare of the New York spotlight, there must be heroes or villains. McAdoo would have been the hero if the Knicks had done well. But they didn't, so he became a villain.

It might be guessed McAdoo regrets leaving Buffalo, but financial security is even more important to him than recognition. And he did not feel he could attain that goal in Buffalo. Snyder offered him an annual salary of $500,000, but much of it was to be in deferred payments.

"I might be dead by 1988 or the club might fold," McAdoo said. "I know a lot of guys who were promised money in the ABA, but the league went under and they got nothing.

"I don't want to play 10 or 11 hard years and then have nothing. I only want security for my family. That's what is important to me. My father has worked hard all his life and has nothing to show for it. That has served as an example for me.

"I would have to consider myself one of the top players in the league and I would like to get paid as one of the top players."

To help make sure he's paid what he's worth, while saving money at the same time, the tight-fisted McAdoo has encouraged his wife, Brenda, to attend law school. That way he won't have to pay an agent's fee.

The New York Knicks and McAdoo can get off to a new start this season and the high-scoring center could become the toast of the town, but winning is a must.

The Knicks and McAdoo were fortunate to escape a lot of criticism last year because so many critics were paying more attention to the Philadelphia 76ers.

"Why's everyone getting on us so much?" 76ers forward George McGinnis had said. "At least we're sure to make the playoffs. Look at all the high-priced talent the Knicks have and they might not even make it."

That's why the heat's on this year, especially for McAdoo.

Blazer Glory

It was, in its own way, a victory for the poor country bumpkin over the rich, sophisticated city slicker. It was Slippery Rock beating Notre Dame in the Rose Bowl. It was Farrah Fawcett-Majors rejecting the Six Million Dollar Man and running away with the neighborhood butcher.

For most of America it was pure ecstasy, one of the more popular upsets since Richard Nixon admitted he made a mistake.

Here was Philadelphia, boasting some of the finest talent ever assembled on a basketball team and with a payroll to match, going in the NBA championship finals against a Portland team which never before had turned in a winning record, which never before had even qualified for the playoffs and which, believe it or not, had finished in the Pacific Division cellar in five of the previous six years.

Indeed, about the only thing the Trail Blazers had led the league in before was anti-establishment statements.

The 76ers were the highest paid team in basketball with an annual payroll of $2.5-million, almost double what Portland's undistinguished crew was earning. At least five of the Philadelphia players—Julius Erving, George McGinnis, Doug Collins, Darryl Dawkins and Caldwell Jones—reportedly have multi-year contracts worth in excess of a million dollars and even the coach, Gene Shue, earns about $200,000 a year.

On the other side of the court, where only Bill Walton was in the super salary structure with a contract calling for more than $2-million, the other Portland players still had to worry about such mundane matters as collecting a decent check and paying their bills.

It was the glaring stars of the galaxy against the working class, and when it was over the bright lights had gone out. The Portland Trail Blazers, after dropping the first two games, took the next four in startling ease to win the NBA championship and introduce a new expression to the sporting public—Blazermania.

It was, in a way, almost as unlikely as you winning the million dollar lottery.

"Some people didn't even know who we were when the playoffs started," said power forward Maurice Lucas, who joined the Blazers from the ABA. "Sure, they knew Bill Walton, but they didn't know us as a team. Well, they may be surprised now, but I'm not. After 109 games, how can I be surprised? We've just accomplished our goal."

Walton, of course, was the big man. After two disappointing years of countless injuries and inflammatory remarks, Walton settled down to basketball and proved himself as dominating a center as Bill Russell had been for the Celtics.

"Bill Walton has been our leader all the way," Coach Jack Ramsay said after the final game. "He is our team captain in every sense of the word. There is no better player, no more cooperative player, no better person than Bill."

Chimed in Shue, the losing coach, "Bill Walton is the best player for a big man who has ever played the game of basketball. We couldn't contain him. He dominated the middle and that threw us out of our game."

Undoubtedly, Walton recognized the playoffs as a golden opportunity to change his public image. His flaming red hair and beard were cut short, he was more outgoing than before, and he demonstrated the pure emotion of an excited kid when he ripped off his jersey following the final victory and threw it into the crowd.

"I feel good all over," said Walton, who scored and rebounded in double figures in all six games of the championship series and was selected as the playoff MVP. "I'm real happy. This was a nice way to win it. It was an exciting game, a good one for me and our team."

The 6-11 center said the NBA title was more meaningful than the two NCAA championship teams he was part of at UCLA because "this championship involves all the best players in this country, playing in one league. With the merger it's truly the first championship of all the United States."

As outstanding as Walton was, the single most important factor was the Blazers' team concept. As Walton put it, "Basically, what went wrong for Philadelphia was that we were a better team. I think we worked harder than everyone else and deserved to win." He later added, "We're not into stardom here."

Erving, the only one of the 76ers to play up to his reputation, and a 40-point scorer in the final game, accepted the loss with good grace although he wasn't willing to accept that Portland had better players.

"I still think we have a better team than Portland," he stated. "We have more talent and more depth. But

Portland players help each other out better than we do. They are cohesive. Their consistency enabled them to win. It was a matchup in opposing styles. Theirs won out."

A final epitaph was written by Shue, who said of his group of super egos, "This isn't the easiest team to coach because we have a lot of strong-willed individuals."

Almost two months before they were to earn $23,750 per man for winning the championship, the Trail Blazers came perilously close to being bounced out of the playoffs before they even started. As the runnerup team in the Pacific Division, Portland had to meet the Chicago Bulls in a preliminary round series.

With Lucas hitting 14 of 17 floor shots for 29 points, the Blazers won the opening game of the best-of-three set, 96-93, but they dropped the second game at Chicago, 107-104, as Artis Gilmore led the Bulls with 27 points.

This left it to a single game and the Blazers, on their home court, ran off to a 16-point lead in the third quarter. But Chicago narrowed the margin to 100-98 on a basket by Jack Marin with only 36 seconds left to play, and at that point the decision could have gone either way, particularly since both Walton and Lucas had fouled out.

Lionel Hollins got the crucial bucket for Portland on an 18-foot jumper with 15 seconds to go, however, and the Blazers clinched a 106-98 triumph as Bob Gross, who led the team with 26 points, and Hollins each converted a pair of free throws.

"My young team is maturing," beamed Ramsay. "That second game in Chicago did a lot for us in learning how to react in a tough situation in front of a huge crowd. It brought us maturity."

In what would prove far more prophetic than anyone imagined at the time, Chicago Coach Ed Badger commented, "I think Portland is going to go a long way in the playoffs."

Two of the other preliminary round series also were stretched to three games, with the Washington Bullets besting the Cleveland Cavaliers and the Golden State Warriors eliminating the Detroit Pistons. In the other set, the Boston Celtics wiped out the San Antonio Spurs in two games.

The early rounds of the playoffs were marked by the presence of pickup referees, since all but two of the regular refs were on strike, and—perhaps coincidentally—by more bickering and scuffling than usual.

All four conference semifinals were extremely competitive, and each deserved a showcase presentation that could only be saved for the league finals. The best pairings matched long-time antagonists Philadelphia and Boston and California rivals Los Angeles and Golden State. Each of those series went the distance, and in both cases home court made the difference as the 76ers and Lakers persevered.

In the other match-ups, former ABA powerhouse Denver made its NBA playoff debut against the young and aggressive Trail Blazers, and perennial playoff contender Washington went against another scrappy team, the Houston Rockets. Portland and Houston were the survivors here, each requiring six games.

Philadelphia vs. Boston was a natural. They play in the same division, and they had had some wild playoff duels in the past, particularly when it was Bill Russell against Wilt Chamberlain. To add further fuel, the Celtics once again were defending champions while the 76ers were rated the favorites to dethrone them.

As the series progressed the bitterness became so

intense that, prior to the fifth game, Philadelphia's 6-11, 250-pound Darryl Dawkins, only 20 years old, said, "To play them you have got to be mean and nasty. I can play that way, too. We aren't supposed to hurt each other, but nastiness is another thing. I'm going to be nasty."

That the Celtics were pumped up for an upset became evident in the first game when they took away the home court advantage by winning at Philadelphia, 113-111. After Julius Erving, who led all scorers with 36 points, missed two foul shots with eight seconds remaining, Jo Jo White hit a 20-foot jump shot at the buzzer to provide the margin of victory.

Noting that Boston had trailed by 13 points in the first half, 76er guard Doug Collins said, "The Celtics die hard. They never give an inch but just keep working hard. They're a smart ballclub."

Philadelphia, a very good ballclub, came back to win the next two games, 113-101 and 109-100, but the Celtics, with Dave Cowens scoring 37 points and grabbing 21 rebounds, drew even with a 124-119 home court victory in which the two substitute referees were the biggest losers. Both teams verbally attacked the two men, Joe Crawford and Richie Jackson; losing Coach Gene Shue protested the game and winning Coach Tom Heinsohn called it "the most incredibly poorly officiated game I have ever seen."

With perfect timing, it was at this point that the referees' strike was settled, and with this no longer an issue the 76ers ran away with the fifth game, 110-91, to take a 3-2 lead. But Jo Jo White scored a career playoff high of 40 points to lead the Celtics to a 113-108 triumph in the sixth game. "If they win the series," White said, "I don't want them to win it in our place."

Only once in a history that includes 13 championships had the Celtics lost the seventh game of a playoff series, but this proud heritage was of little value before 18,276 screaming fans in the Spectrum when Philadelphia won the decisive game, 83-77. Lloyd Free, who led all scorers with 27 points, danced away the final five seconds of play, explaining later, "That's right, that was the boogaloo. That's what the Celtics did to us when they won the first game here. They humiliated us, and that's what I wanted to do to them. Today was our turn."

Erving was more level-headed following the victory. "This is just one hurdle of the three that have to be crossed to get to the top. I doubt if any other series can be as tough as this one, but we'll just have to wait and see."

Los Angeles, after compiling a 53-29 record, the best of any NBA team, in the regular season under rookie Coach Jerry West, had the home court advantage in its series against Golden State. That and the presence of league MVP Kareem Abdul-Jabbar proved to be the deciding factors as the home team won each game.

Abdul-Jabbar, despite a migraine headache, scored 27 points in LA's 115-106 opening game triumph and he had 40 points, 19 rebounds and nine blocked shots as the Lakers took the second contest, 95-86.

Jamaal Wilkes of the Warriors said of Abdul-Jabbar, "He is playing the greatest basketball of his life. There's nothing we can do."

Actually, Golden State did figure out something. It went home and evened the series as Rick Barry had 40 and 26 point games. Not even a 41-point performance by Abdul-Jabbar in the fourth game could prevent the Lakers from taking a 114-103 bath.

Returning home, Los Angeles had a pleasant surprise waiting when guard Lucius Allen, who had dislocated a toe in the first game, returned to the lineup. Abdul-Jabbar scored 45 points and pulled down 18 rebounds as LA won, 112-105, then credited Allen, a fellow UCLA alumnus. "You can't measure what Lucius means to us," he said. "He's pulled us together at times when we would have scattered the way we did in Oakland. He slows us down and makes us play smart."

The Warriors, who haven't lost to Los Angeles at home since 1973, kept alive that hex—and their season—by winning the sixth game, 115-106, despite 43 points by Abdul-Jabbar.

Golden State steamed to a 32-18 lead in the deciding seventh game when the series and the season turned around on one intemperate act by rookie Robert Parish. The 7-foot center shoved his elbow into Abdul-Jabbar's face, causing the Laker star to whip off the protective mask he wears over his glasses and angrily throw the ball out of bounds.

Virtually harmless till that point, Abdul-Jabbar erupted for 10 points in the next 10 minutes to lift the Lakers into a 48-46 halftime lead, and he wound up with 36 points and 26 rebounds as LA won, 97-84.

"He [Parish] was trying to play tough defense," Abdul-Jabbar said. "He was crowding me and bumping me. When I was trying to go across the middle, we just got tangled up and we started flailing a few elbows. But it died right there."

And so did Golden State.

Houston won three of four regular season games from Washington and beat out the Bullets by one game for the Central Division crown. But the Rockets couldn't come close to matching the playoff experience of their rivals. In fact, Washington center Wes Unseld had played more minutes in playoffs than the entire Rocket roster combined.

So much for experience. After dropping the opener, 111-101, to lose their home court advantage, the Rockets won four of the next five contests, including two in a row at Washington.

In the sixth game, Mike Newlin scored 15 of his 21 points in the final quarter to lift Houston to a 108-103 victory. Rudy Tomjanovich led all scorers with 26 points, but through the series it was big Moses Malone who made the difference for the Rockets.

"He's the great equalizer underneath," said Washington Coach Dick Motta. "Even if they miss those shots, there's a pretty good chance he can get the rebound, or at least tip it and keep it alive."

Denver, which tied Philadelphia at 50-32 for the second best record in the NBA, threw away this advantage by dropping the opening game at home to Portland, 101-100, on a twisting jump shot by Maurice Lucas with 11 seconds remaining. The Nuggets won the next meeting, 121-111, but the damage had been done.

The Blazers had compiled a 35-6 record at home, and as Denver Coach Larry Brown put it, "Portland may be the toughest city in the league in which to win because of the fans there."

Whatever the reason, the Blazers wrapped up the series with three victories at home. Their second loss was in overtime, at Denver.

"We want the Lakers now," Ramsay, the Portland coach, said even before the LA-Golden State series had ended. "I kind of think my players would like to play them just to prove we can beat them."

To some, this may have sounded like a death wish. Portland had beaten the Warriors three of four times in the regular season, and would have had the extra home game in a series against them. On the other hand, the Blazers had lost three of four to LA, and the Lakers were due for the home court advantage. Indeed, Los Angeles had set an NBA regular season record by winning 37 of 41 games at the Forum, including 21 in a row.

But Portland knew enough about these home court hexes to be able to deal with them. In a classic confrontation matching Walton against Abdul-Jabbar, the Blazers shocked Los Angeles by winning the first two games at the Forum. Abdul-Jabbar scored 30 points in the opening 121-109 setback, but was neutralized by Walton's 22 points, 13 rebounds and six assists. In the second game, Abdul-Jabbar outscored Walton 40-14, with each man clearing 17 rebounds, but again it was Portland on top, 99-97.

With the series returning to Portland, there were very few who doubted that the Blazers would win the series. It seemed to come down to a matter of whether LA could salvage one game on the road and avoid a sweep. It couldn't.

Walton scored 14 points in the final quarter of game three to assure a 102-97 victory, and Portland then wound it up, 105-101, as Lucas scored 26 points.

Jerry West credited Portland's speed for its overwhelming success. "That was the whole difference in the series, their quickness. Kareem did everything humanly possible to win a basketball game, but we couldn't give him the help he needed. Walton is a magnificent center, but they also knew how to help him, with a great power forward in Lucas and that backcourt speed."

It was in the Eastern Conference final that people were talking about the prospects of a sweep since Philadelphia seemed too strong for Houston. And, for a while, it appeared a likely prophecy as the 76ers took the first two games, 128-117 and 106-97. The Rocket front line of 7-foot Kevin Kunnert and 6-8 Rudy Tomjanovich was unable to keep up with Erving and McGinnis, causing Coach Tom Nissalke to say that he'd freeze the ball if it wasn't for the 24-second clock.

However, Houston found a new life on its home court, routing the 76ers, 118-94. Calvin Murphy, the Rockets' 5-9 guard, said, "We have a lot of pride. They were talking about sweeping. Hell, that made me mad. We may just sweep them in six."

Pride notwithstanding, the 76ers took a commanding 3-1 lead by winning the next game at Houston, 107-95, and looked like they would wrap it up at home when they raced to a 17-point lead in the third quarter. But the Rockets refused to fizzle and came back to win, 118-115, with rookie John Lucas putting them ahead for good with 1:34 left.

"It became too easy for us, just too easy," moaned McGinnis. "For some reason, we lost our intensity when we got the lead. We thought they were going to die, but they didn't."

The 76ers finally clinched their berth in the finals the hard way, winning the sixth game before a hostile sellout crowd at Houston, 112-109. Helping Philadelphia considerably was a charging call on Lucas by referee Jake O'Donnell with eight seconds to go. This nullified a basket which would have tied the game at 111-all.

"As much as they are known for their individual talent, it was interesting that in the final quarter they had to run a pattern to get points," said Nissalke. "And when that didn't work, I could hear them say, 'Hey, Doctor, where are you?'" The Doctor, Julius Erving, scored a game-high 34 points.

Present at the final game was Jack Ramsay, who

had coached the 76ers four years and also had spent 11 years at St. Joseph's College in Philadelphia. Therefore, it came as no surprise when he revealed which team he wanted to meet for the championship.

"I wanted Philadelphia to win," the Portland coach said, "because Philly is the wonder team and we want a chance to beat the best."

There was no question that Philadelphia, with all its well-paid talent, belonged in the finals. But the Blazers? Aside from Bill Walton and the powerful Maurice Lucas, they were a team without a reputation. Dave Twardzik, Lloyd Neal, Bob Gross, Herm Gilliam, Corky Calhoun, Larry Steele, Lionel Hollins, Johnny Davis, Wally Walker—to most fans, particularly in the eastern half of the country, they were merely names on a roster.

But they believed in themselves, and knew what they had to do.

"Philadelphia probably has more talent, more superstars, than anybody in the league," Ramsay said. "I think we have to shut down their three big guns [Erving, McGinnis and Collins] as well as we can.

"Our series will be one of contrasting styles. They do a lot of one-on-one plays whereas we're more team-oriented. But they're very good at one-on-one."

In the opener, Portland managed to contain McGinnis, who was mired in a playoff-long slump anyway, but could do little with Erving and Collins, who scored 33 and 30 points, respectively, to power Philadelphia to a 107-101 victory. The Blazers, who had been idle eight days, didn't help themselves as they committed 34 turnovers.

In speaking of his performance, Erving said, "It's all game preparation. You have to be ready to play. In this situation, you don't want to lose a game you could have won.

"My concentration on offense is more profound in the playoffs than during the season. Also, the adrenalin for these games does cause a chemical reaction in your body."

Gross, who had the almost impossible assignment of trying to stop Erving, commented, "I've got to play him tougher. You can't let him get the ball where he wants it. You try to keep the ball away from him. He's not only a great shooter, he's a smart player."

Collins came back with 27 points and Erving with 20 as Philadelphia easily won the second game, 107-89, but Erving made a statement that eventually would haunt him: "People think we're a bunch of renegades. They think a well-drilled team can come in here and pick us apart. Well, we're proving them wrong."

These words, as well as most of the game, were overshadowed by a brawl that broke out with 4:52 left. The principals were Dawkins and Lucas, who carry some 460 pounds between them. About 100 fans raced onto the court, but the only casualty was Collins, who was hit accidentally by Dawkins near his right eye and required four stitches. Lucas and Dawkins later were fined $2500 each by NBA Commissioner Larry O'Brien.

When the teams moved on to Portland, there were more than a few 76er fans who believed the clubs wouldn't have to return to Philadelphia for a fifth game. The Blazers didn't look anything like prospective champions and as Ramsay put it, "We have not played poised basketball."

Still, Lucas warned, "We'll see them in Portland. We are a long way from dead."

Ramsay said the key for the Blazers is "to own a lead so as to be in position to command the game," and this is just what his club proceeded to do the rest of the series. In the third game it was a 34-21 surge in the opening period that carried Portland to a 129-107 triumph, and in the fourth game, after running up a 29-16 lead in the first quarter, the Blazers went on a 41-point tear in the third period for a 130-98 rout.

Hollins, who scored 25 points in the equalizer, admitted, "When we came home from Philadelphia, I wasn't sure we could beat them. Now I know we can."

There was still one difficult obstacle for Portland to overcome. As expressed by Ramsay, "We've really been playing our game at home. Now we have to win one in Philadelphia if we want to win the championship. They still have the home court advantage and we have to turn that around somewhere along the way."

Having found the formula, the Blazers capitalized in the key fifth game, taking control by running off to a 22-15 lead in the opening quarter, then wrapping up matters with another 40-point third quarter outburst. Typical of the Portland attack, six players scored in double figures, led by Gross with 25 points. Erving had 37 points for Philadelphia.

"We knew we could beat them," Lucas said, "It's not just talk. We came out and we did it. It's the mark of a good team to keep your poise."

With the Blazers returning home (where they were greeted at the airport by an estimated 5000 fans at 4:30 in the morning), Hollins said, "It's in our hands now. Now we'll see how badly we want it. Opportunity for us to be a champion is there, but we can't afford to take them lightly."

There was no way the Trail Blazers were going to let up now, and for the fourth consecutive time they took the initiative, racing off to a 67-55 halftime advantage. With McGinnis having his first good game of the series, scoring 28 points, the 76ers clawed back to within two points in the closing seconds, but Erving, Lloyd Free and McGinnis all missed shots.

The final score was 109-107, making the Blazers the first team ever to win four games in a row in the championship finals after dropping the first two.

"Bill Walton is the finest player for a big man who has ever played the game of basketball," marveled Shue. "We couldn't contain him. He dominated the middle, and that threw us out of our game."

Declared Ramsay, "This is the finest team and the finest people I've ever coached. This is what I've aimed for since becoming a professional coach, but I would feel the same way and say the same thing about these players even if we hadn't won."

Hall of Records

A reference section of National Basketball Association statistics

Hall of Records

NBA CHAMPIONS OVER THE YEARS

Season	Champion	Eastern Division	W.	L.	Western Division	W.	L.
1946-47	Philadelphia	Philadelphia	49	11	Chicago	39	22
1947-48	Baltimore	Philadelphia	27	21	St. Louis	29	19
1948-49	Minneapolis	Washington	38	22	Rochester	45	15
1949-50	Minneapolis	Syracuse	51	13	*Indianapolis	39	25
1950-51	Rochester	Philadelphia	40	26	Minneapolis	44	24
1951-52	Minneapolis	Syracuse	40	26	Rochester	41	25
1952-53	Minneapolis	New York	47	23	Minneapolis	48	22
1953-54	Minneapolis	New York	44	28	Minneapolis	46	26
1954-55	Syracuse	Syracuse	43	29	Ft. Wayne	43	29
1955-56	Philadelphia	Philadelphia	45	27	Ft. Wayne	37	35
1956-57	Boston	Boston	44	28	StL-Mpl-FtW	34	38
1957-58	St. Louis	Boston	49	23	St. Louis	41	31
1958-59	Boston	Boston	52	20	St. Louis	49	23
1959-60	Boston	Boston	59	16	St. Louis	46	29
1960-61	Boston	Boston	57	22	St. Louis	51	28
1961-62	Boston	Boston	60	20	Los Angeles	54	26
1962-63	Boston	Boston	58	22	Los Angeles	53	27
1963-64	Boston	Boston	59	21	San Fran.	48	32
1964-65	Boston	Boston	62	18	Los Angeles	49	31
1965-66	Boston	Philadelphia	55	25	Los Angeles	45	35
1966-67	Philadelphia	Philadelphia	68	13	San Fran.	44	37
1967-68	Boston	Philadelphia	62	20	St. Louis	56	26
1968-69	Boston	Baltimore	57	25	Los Angeles	55	27
1969-70	New York	New York	60	22	Atlanta	48	34
1970-71	Milwaukee	Baltimore	42	40	Milwaukee	66	16
1971-72	Los Angeles	New York	48	34	Los Angeles	69	13
1972-73	New York	Boston	68	14	L.A.-Milwaukee	60	22
1973-74	Boston	Boston	56	26	Milwaukee	59	23
1974-75	Golden State	Washington	60	22	Golden State	48	34
1975-76	Boston	Boston	54	28	Phoenix	42	40
1976-77	Portland	Philadelphia	50	32	Portland	49	33

* 1949-50 Central Division Champ: Minneapolis and Rochester tied 51-17.

HALL OF RECORDS

NBA STATISTICAL LEADERS

Season	Fg Pct. Leaders		FT Pct. Leaders		Top Rebounders	
1946-47	Bob Feerick (Wash.)	.401	Fred Scolari (Wash.)	.811		
1947-48	Bob Feerick (Wash.)	.340	Bob Feerick (Wash.)	.788		
1948-49	Arnie Risen (Roch.)	.423	Bob Feerick (Wash.)	.859		
1949-50	Alex Groza (Indpls.)	.478	Max Zaslofsky (Chi.)	.843		
1950-51	Alex Groza (Indpls.)	.470	Joe Fulks (Phil.)	.855	1080	Dolph Schayes (Syr.)
1951-52	Paul Arizin (Phil.)	.448	Bob Wanzer (Roch.)	.904	880	Larry Foust (Ft. W.) / Mel Hutchins (Mil.)
1952-53	Neil Johnston (Phil.)	.452	Bill Sharman (Bos.)	.850	1007	George Mikan (Mpls.)
1953-54	Ed Macauley (Boston)	.486	Bill Sharman (Bos.)	.844	1098	Harry Gallatin (N.Y.)
1954-55	Larry Foust (Ft. W.)	.487	Bill Sharman (Bos.)	.897	1085	Neil Johnston (Phil.)
1955-56	Neil Johnston (Phil.)	.457	Bill Sharman (Bos.)	.867	1164	Bob Pettit (St. Louis)
1956-57	Neil Johnston (Phil.)	.447	Bill Sharman (Bos.)	.905	1256	Maurice Stokes (Roch.)
1957-58	Jack Twyman (Cinn.)	.452	Dolph Schayes (Syr.)	.904	1564	Bill Russell (Boston)
1958-59	Ken Sears (N.Y.)	.490	Bill Sharman (Bos.)	.932	1612	Bill Russell (Boston)
1959-60	Ken Sears (N.Y.)	.477	Dolph Schayes (Syr.)	.892	1941	Wilt Chamberlain (Phil.)
1960-61	Wilt Chamberlain (Phil.)	.505	Bill Sharman (Bos.)	.921	2149	Wilt Chamberlain (Phil.)
1961-62	Walt Bellamy (Chi.)	.513	Dolph Schayes (Syr.)	.896	2052	Wilt Chamberlain (Phil.)
1962-63	Wilt Chamberlain (S.F.)	.528	Larry Costello (Syr.)	.881	1946	Wilt Chamberlain (S.F.)
1963-64	Jerry Lucas (Cinn.)	.527	Oscar Robertson (Cinn.)	.853	1930	Bill Russell (Boston)
1964-65	Wilt Cham'ain (S.F.-Phil.)	.510	Larry Costello (Phil.)	.877	1878	Bill Russell (Boston)
1965-66	Wilt Chamberlain (Phil.)	.540	Larry Siegfried (Bos.)	.881	1943	Wilt Chamberlain (Phil.)
1966-67	Wilt Chamberlain (Phil.)	.683	Adrian Smith (Cinn.)	.903	1957	Wilt Chamberlain (Phil.)
1967-68	Wilt Chamberlain (Phil.)	.595	Oscar Robertson (Cinn.)	.873	1952	Wilt Chamberlain (Phil.)
1968-69	Wilt Chamberlain (L.A.)	.583	Larry Siegfried (Bos.)	.864	1712	Wilt Chamberlain (L.A.)
1969-70	Johnny Green (Cinn.)	.559	Flynn Robinson (Mil.)	.898	16.9*	Elvin Hayes (S.D.)
1970-71	Johnny Green (Cinn.)	.587	Chet Walker (Chi.)	.859	18.2*	Wilt Chamberlain (L.A.)
1971-72	Wilt Chamberlain (L.A.)	.649	Jack Marin (Balt.)	.894	19.2*	Wilt Chamberlain (L.A.)
1972-73	Wilt Chamberlain (L.A.)	.727	Rick Barry (Gol. St.)	.902	18.6*	Wilt Chamberlain (L.A.)
1973-74	Bob McAdoo (Buf.)	.547	Ernie DiGregorio (Buf.)	.902	18.1*	Elvin Hayes (Cap.)
1974-75	Don Nelson (Boston)	.539	Rick Barry (Gol. St.)	.904	14.8*	Wes Unseld (Wash.)
1975-76	Wes Unseld (Wash.)	.561	Rick Barry (Gol. St.)	.920	16.9*	Kareem Abdul-Jabbar (L.A.)
1976-77	Kareem Abdul-Jabbar (L.A.)	.579	Ernie DiGregorio (Buf.)	.945	14.4*	Bill Walton (Port.)

* Based on highest average per game.

HALL OF RECORDS

Season	Most Assists	No.	Most Minutes	No.	Most Personals	No.
1946-47	Ernie Calverly (Prov.)	202			Stan Mlasek (Detroit)	208
1947-48	Howie Dallmar (Phil.)	120			Charles Gilmur (Chi.)	231
1948-49	Bob Davies (Roch.)	321			Ed Sadowski (Phil.)	273
1949-50	Dick McGuire (N.Y.)	386			George Mikan (Mpls.)	297
1950-51	Andy Phillip (Phil.)	414			George Mikan (Mpls.)	308
1951-52	Andy Phillip (Phil.)	539	Paul Arizin (Phil.)	2939	George Mikan (Mpls.)	286
1952-53	Bob Cousy (Boston)	547	Neil Johnston (Phil.)	3166	Don Meineke (Ft. W.)	334
1953-54	Bob Cousy (Boston)	578	Neil Johnston (Phil.)	3296	Earl Lloyd (Syracuse)	303
1954-55	Bob Cousy (Boston)	557	Paul Arizin (Phil.)	2953	Vern Mikkelsen (Mpls.)	319
1955-56	Bob Cousy (Boston)	642	Slater Martin (Mpls.)	2838	Vern Mikkelsen (Mpls.)	319
1956-57	Bob Cousy (Boston)	478	Dolph Schayes (Syr.)	2851	Vern Mikkelsen (Mpls.)	312
1957-58	Bob Cousy (Boston)	463	Dolph Schayes (Syr.)	2918	Walt Dukes (Detroit)	311
1958-59	Bob Cousy (Boston)	557	Bill Russell (Boston)	2979	Walt Dukes (Detroit)	332
1959-60	Bob Cousy (Boston)	715			Tom Gola (Phil.)	311
1960-61	Oscar Robertson (Cinn.)	690	Wilt Chamberlain (Phil.) { Gene Shue (Detroit)	3338 3773	Paul Arizin (Phil.)	335
1961-62	Oscar Robertson (Cinn.)	899	Wilt Chamberlain (Phil.)	3882	Walt Dukes (Detroit)	327
1962-63	Guy Rodgers (S.F.)	825	Wilt Chamberlain (S.F.)	3802	Tom Gola (S.F.-N.Y.)	316
1963-64	Oscar Robertson (Cinn.)	868	Wilt Chamberlain (S.F.)	3689	Wayne Embry (Cinn.)	325
1964-65	Oscar Robertson (Cinn.)	861	Bill Russell (Boston)	3466	Bailey Howell (Balt.)	345
1965-66	Oscar Robertson (Cinn.)	847	Wilt Chamberlain (Phil.)	3737	Zelmo Beaty (St. Louis)	344
1966-67	Guy Rodgers (Chi.)	908	Wilt Chamberlain (Phil.)	3682	Joe Strawder (Detroit)	344
1967-68	Wilt Chamberlain (Phil.)	702	Wilt Chamberlain (Phil.)	3836	Bill Bridges (St. Louis)	366
1968-69	Oscar Robertson (Cinn.)	772	Wilt Chamberlain (Phil.)	3695	Billy Cunningham (Phil.)	329
1969-70	9.1* Len Wilkens (Sea.)		Elvin Hayes (S.D.)	3665	Jim Davis (Atlanta)	335
1970-71	10.1* Norm Van Lier (Cinn.)		Elvin Hayes (S.D.)	3678	Dave Cowens (Boston)	350
1971-72	9.7* Jerry West (L.A.)		John Havlicek (Bos.)	3698	Dave Cowens (Boston)	314
1972-73	11.4* Nate Archibald (K.C.-O.)		John Havlicek (Bos.)	3681	Neal Walk (Phoenix)	323
1973-74	8.2* Ernie DiGregorio (Buf.)		Nate Archibald (K.C.-O.)	3602	Kevin Porter (Cap.)	319
1974-75	8.0* Kevin Porter (Wash.)		Bob McAdoo (Buf.)	3539	{Phil Jackson (N.Y.) Bob Dandridge (Milwaukee)	330
1975-76	8.1* Don Watts (Sea.)		Kareem Abdul-Jabbar (L.A.)	3379	Charlie Scott (Bos.)	356
1976-77	8.5* Don Buse (Ind.)		Elvin Hayes (Wash.)	3364	Lonnie Shelton (N.Y.K.)	363

* Based on highest average per game

MOST POINTS SCORED IN ONE GAME
(IN REGULAR-SEASON PLAY)

	FG.	F.	Pts.
Wilt Chamberlain, Philadelphia vs. New York at Hershey, Pa., March 2, 1962	36	28	100
Wilt Chamberlain, Philadelphia vs. Los Angeles at Philadelphia, December 8, 1961 ***	31	16	78
Wilt Chamberlain, Philadelphia vs. Chicago at Philadelphia, January 13, 1962	29	15	73
Wilt Chamberlain, San Francisco at New York, November 16, 1962	29	15	73
Wilt Chamberlain, San Francisco at Los Angeles, November 3, 1962	29	14	72
Elgin Baylor, Los Angeles at New York, November 15, 1960	28	15	71
Wilt Chamberlain, San Francisco at Syracuse, March 10, 1963	27	16	70
Wilt Chamberlain, Philadelphia at Chicago, December 16, 1967	30	8	68
Pete Maravich, New Orleans vs. N.Y. Knicks at New York, February 25, 1977	26	16	68
Wilt Chamberlain, Philadelphia vs. New York at Philadelphia, March 9, 1961	27	13	67
Wilt Chamberlain, Philadelphia at St. Louis, February 17, 1962	26	15	67
Wilt Chamberlain, Philadelphia vs. New York at Philadelphia, February 26, 1962	25	17	67
Wilt Chamberlain, San Francisco vs. Los Angeles at San Francisco, January 17, 1963	28	11	67
Wilt Chamberlain, Los Angeles at Phoenix, February 9, 1969	29	8	66
Wilt Chamberlain, Philadelphia at Cincinnati, February 13, 1962	24	17	65
Wilt Chamberlain, Philadelphia at St. Louis, February 27, 1962	25	15	65
Wilt Chamberlain, Philadelphia vs. Los Angeles at Philadelphia, February 7, 1966	28	9	65
Elgin Baylor, Minneapolis vs. Boston, November 8, 1959	25	14	64
Rick Barry, Golden State vs. Portland at San Francisco, March 26, 1974	30	4	64
Joe Fulks, Philadelphia vs. Indianapolis at Philadelphia, February 10, 1949	27	9	63
Elgin Baylor, Los Angeles at Philadelphia, December 8, 1961 ***	23	17	63
Jerry West, Los Angeles vs. New York at Los Angeles, January 17, 1962	22	19	63
Wilt Chamberlain, San Francisco vs. Los Angeles at San Francisco, December 14, 1962	24	15	63
Wilt Chamberlain, San Francisco at Philadelphia, November 26, 1964	27	9	63
Wilt Chamberlain, Philadelphia at Boston, January 14, 1962	27	8	62
Wilt Chamberlain, Philadelphia vs. St. Louis at Detroit, January 17, 1962 *	24	14	62
Wilt Chamberlain, Philadelphia vs. Syracuse at Utica, New York, January 21, 1962 *	25	12	62
Wilt Chamberlain, San Francisco at New York, January 29, 1963	27	8	62
Wilt Chamberlain, San Francisco at Cincinnati, November 15, 1964	26	10	62
Wilt Chamberlain, Philadelphia vs. San Francisco at Philadelphia, March 3, 1966	26	10	62

* Denotes each overtime period played.

HALL OF RECORDS 215

MOST FIELD GOALS SCORED IN ONE GAME
(IN REGULAR-SEASON PLAY)

	FGA.	FGM.
Wilt Chamberlain, Philadelphia vs. New York at Hershey, Pa., March 2, 1962	63	36
Wilt Chamberlain, Philadelphia vs. Los Angeles at Philadelphia, December 8, 1961	62***	31
Wilt Chamberlain, Philadelphia at Chicago, December 16, 1967	40	30
Wilt Chamberlain, Los Angeles at Phoenix, February 9, 1969	35	29
Wilt Chamberlain, Philadelphia vs. Chicago at Philadelphia, January 13, 1962	48	29
Wilt Chamberlain, San Francisco at Los Angeles, November 3, 1962	48	29
Wilt Chamberlain, San Francisco at New York, November 16, 1962	43	29
Elgin Baylor, Los Angeles at New York, November 15, 1960	48	28
Wilt Chamberlain, Philadelphia vs. Chicago at Philadelphia, December 9, 1961	48	28
Wilt Chamberlain, San Francisco vs. Los Angeles at San Francisco, January 11, 1963	47	28
Wilt Chamberlain, Philadelphia vs. Los Angeles at Philadelphia, February 7, 1966	43	28
Joe Fulks, Philadelphia vs. Indianapolis at Philadelphia, February 10, 1949	56	27
Wilt Chamberlain, Philadelphia vs. New York at Philadelphia, March 9, 1961	37	27
Wilt Chamberlain, Philadelphia at Boston, January 14, 1962	45	27
Wilt Chamberlain, San Francisco vs. Cincinnati at San Francisco, November 21, 1962	52	27
Wilt Chamberlain, San Francisco vs. Syracuse at San Francisco, December 11, 1962	57	27
Wilt Chamberlain, San Francisco at New York, January 29, 1963	44	27
Wilt Chamberlain, San Francisco at Syracuse, March 10, 1963	38	27
Wilt Chamberlain, San Francisco at Philadelphia, November 26, 1964	58	27
Wilt Chamberlain, Philadelphia at New York, February 21, 1960	47	26
Wilt Chamberlain, Philadelphia at St. Louis, February 17, 1962	44	26
Wilt Chamberlain, San Francisco vs. St. Louis at San Francisco, December 18, 1962	53**	26
Wilt Chamberlain, San Francisco at Los Angeles, February 16, 1963	47	26
Wilt Chamberlain, San Francisco at Cincinnati, November 15, 1964	44	26
Wilt Chamberlain, Philadelphia vs. San Francisco at Philadelphia, March 3, 1966	39	26
Wilt Chamberlain, Philadelphia vs. Cincinnati at Philadelphia, February 13, 1967	34	26
Pete Maravich, New Orleans vs. N.Y. Knicks at New Orleans, February 25, 1977	43	26

* Denotes each overtime period played.

HALL OF RECORDS

MOST FREE THROWS MADE IN ONE GAME
(IN REGULAR-SEASON PLAY)

	FTA.	FTM.
Wilt Chamberlain, Philadelphia vs. New York at Hershey, Pa., March 2, 1962	32	28
Frank Selvy, Milwaukee vs. Minneapolis at Ft. Wayne, December 2, 1954	26	24
Dolph Schayes, Syracuse vs. Minneapolis at Syracuse, January 17, 1952	27 ***	23
Nate Archibald, Cincinnati vs. Detroit at Cincinnati, February 5, 1973	* 24	23
Pete Maravich, New Orleans vs. New York at New Orleans, October 27, 1975	** 26	23

* Denotes each overtime period played.

MOST REBOUNDS IN ONE GAME
(IN REGULAR-SEASON PLAY)

	Reb.
Wilt Chamberlain, Philadelphia vs. Boston at Philadelphia, November 24, 1960	55
Bill Russell, Boston vs. Syracuse at Boston, February 8, 1960	51
Bill Russell, Boston vs. Philadelphia at Boston, November 16, 1957	49
Bill Russell, Boston vs. Detroit at Providence, March 11, 1965	49
Wilt Chamberlain, Philadelphia vs. Syracuse at Philadelphia, February 6, 1960	45
Wilt Chamberlain, Philadelphia vs. Los Angeles at Philadelphia, January 21, 1961	45

MOST ASSISTS IN ONE GAME
(IN REGULAR-SEASON PLAY)

	Ast.
Bob Cousy, Boston-Minneapolis at Boston, February 27, 1959	28
Guy Rodgers, San Francisco vs. St. Louis at San Francisco, March 14, 1963	28
Ernie DiGregorio, Buffalo at Portland, January 1, 1974	25
Guy Rodgers, Chicago vs. New York at Chicago, December 20, 1966	24
Jerry West, Los Angeles vs. Philadelphia at Los Angeles, February 1, 1967	23